Coming Home

A Stranger in the Smokies

Written by

John Wade Christensen

SKINNY BROWN DOG
MEDIA
EST. 2013
ATLANTA | PUNTA DEL ESTE

Published by Skinny Brown Dog Media

Atlanta, GA /Punta del Este, Uruguay

http://www.SkinnyBrownDogMedia.com

Copyright © 2023 John Wade Christensen

Distributed by Skinny Brown Dog Media

Design and composition by Skinny Brown Dog Media

Cover Design by Jamie Ty

Library of Congress Cataloging-in-Publication Data Print

ISBN ebook - 978-1-957506-49-4

ISBN paperback - 978-1-957506-48-7

ISBN Hardback 978-1-957506-50-0

Dedication

To Shauna, Kiersten, McRae, Regan and Gryffen

Forgive me for taking so long to pull myself together.

Without you I would not be here.

Acknowledgments

For a short book, this was a long time in coming. I will most likely forget a few people who encouraged and supported me along the way. To them, my apologies. It is not intentional, and this is one occasion where I'll use the excuse of forgetfulness that rides shotgun with aging.

I want to take a moment to acknowledge.

Eric G. Reid of Skinny Brown Dog Media. Eric is an independent publisher. His willingness to take on this project, even with my limited resources, is based simply on a belief in me and this story and his love of the people of the hills. The man is a prince.

This is the second time my friend Bob Land has stepped up as an editor. Again, his eye for detail has been invaluable.

Duane Truex, my brother on the path, thank you for being that little voice on my shoulder who refused to accept any answer other than anything but "Yes, I'm working on it!".

Mary Jane Stafford has been an incredible role model through her mission of providing "hope for the hurting." Thank you for supporting me and my mental health on this book journey.

My brothers Dave, Phil, Paul, and Jeff have loved, supported, and encouraged me, their wayward and seemingly unfocused oldest brother. I wish I'd been a better role model, but there's more where this came from, so there's still hope.

My compadre, Saul Weber, Thank you for my bottle of Herradura Ultra and a handwritten note that said, "Congratulations on your new book." Even if I wasn't close to finishing, in fact, I finished the tequila before the book. However, I did keep the empty bottle where I could see it, reminding me of your faith in me.

Thank you to my spiritual brothers, the parking lot ministry team: Robert, Mike, Mark, Jim W, David Mystery, Jon, Geoff, Barry, JD, Grant, Joel, Jim C. Henry, Mike L, John M., Brian, Sam, Bob T, Palm Beach David. Without you all this book wouldn't exist.

Steve Perras, watching you figure out life the hard way. Or, as in E.F. Hutton's commercial, "he earned it." Every time I am with you, I walk away a rich man.

Being included in the NWPC family has been a blessing. Thank you all, especially Anneke, Henry, Bill, Harry, Nate, Jen and Dan, and the dozen others who have enriched me immeasurably.

Paul Hanna, John Marshall, Lucas Aramian, John Simonds, Steve Spence, Roy Jones, Mike Wilson, Charles David, Mary Katherine, and Mary Antoinette. Thank you for everything you poured into me.

Special Thank you to my Facebook Family, who helped me make so many decisions, from picking a cover and author photo to sorting out a tricky phrase. Too many to mention, but I'm so grateful to them.

Thanks to Jamie Ty and her team for the great cover.

Finally, thank you to the kind, generous people who took me into the Andrews family: Scott, Tony, George, Griff, Ruth, Teresa, Lawrence, Ray, Jo, Jim, and Bob.

With whole heart and deep gratitude, thank you to the people of the Smokies. Jane Brown, you were right when you said the warmth and acceptance I got in Andrews, North Carolina, "has something to do with the mountains."

Contents

Prologue

The idea to write a book came to me shortly after I was laid off in January 2001 in a corporate merger. The premise: that we live in a friendly universe, that despite appearances to the contrary there is a benevolent force behind it all.

Obviously an element of self-interest was involved. I was two months shy of my 56th birthday. My profession—journalism—was going through a ghastly contraction. People were getting buyouts or being laid off. The dot-com bubble was deflating and would be followed by the aptly named Great Recession.

To make matters worse, thanks to poor decisions and a little bad luck, I didn't have much of a financial cushion to fall back on. At an age when many of my peers were easing toward retirement, I was faced with starting over. At a time when millions of others were losing their jobs, I was just another anxious face in the crowd.

But the book idea wasn't only wishful thinking. After difficult years early in life, I became what Don Henley called in one of his songs "a restless spirit on an endless flight." I moved several times, changed jobs, and was always looking for something that would soothe and settle me. Sex, drugs, and rock and roll led eventually to religion and then to other forms of spirituality. I figured I could harvest what I'd learned along the way, include interviews and experiences from my career as a journalist, and sprinkle in a few anecdotes from my unusual personal life.

The problem was that, even in the best of conditions, books are long-term propositions with unpredictable futures. In what were shaping up as hard times, I needed short-term answers and predictable income. So I dropped the book idea and turned my attention elsewhere.

Fortunately I already had a project underway.

My last assignment as a senior writer for CNN.com involved going to the Smoky Mountains to report on the manhunt for the terrorist Eric Rudolph. While working on that assignment, I became interested in the epicenter of the search, the small and seemingly dying town of Andrews, North Carolina.

Despite factories shutting down, businesses closing, and the exodus of a third of its population, the people in Andrews were passionate about the place. Fascinated, I completed the Rudolph assignment and then returned repeatedly over the next 18 months to document a way of life that seemed like a theme park of small-town Americana, a real-life version of Thornton Wilder's classic play, *Our Town*.

When I finished writing, the piece was too long for a magazine but wasn't quite a book. I knew I had something, but I didn't know what was missing. I tucked it away in an accordion folder and began what would be the most difficult and amazing time of my life . . . which hadn't exactly been uneventful to begin with.

I was on a state championship basketball team in high school and made the all-tournament team. I played football in high school and my first year in college. I survived a life-threatening spill in a fast-moving Kentucky river and a 360-degree spin on a rain-slick Honolulu expressway. I was present at shootings at a bar, a concert and a sporting event -- the nightlife trifecta.

I hitchhiked cross-country, broke a board with my hand, body-surfed in thundering mid-Pacific waves, ran a marathon, and walked barefoot across twenty feet of glowing coals (it seemed like a good idea at the time).

I did recreational drugs for thirteen years, quit, and went on a Gulliver's Travels through the New Age 1980s. A former model and Clairol girl introduced me to crystals, psychics, and carrot juice. I hung out with ersatz Sufis, saw Shirley MacLaine at two gatherings (disguise: floppy straw hat, big sunglasses), and spent two weeks in a yoga ashram.

That was during off-duty hours.

As a journalist, I rafted the Ohio River, canoed the Boundary Waters in Minnesota, and kayaked the Na Pali coast of Kauai. I raced a high-performance sports car at Sears Point Raceway in California. I flew 720 miles an hour and experienced zero gravity upside down in the rear seat of an F-4f Phantom fighter jet.

I was arrested covering a demonstration and spent a few hours in jail. I went on a stakeout with pistol-packing Headline News anchor Lynne Russell, who was moonlighting as a private investigator.

Quieter moments included interviewing a Nobel Prize laureate (Linus Pauling); two Pulitzer Prize winners (Leon Edel and W. S. Merwin); two precocious 19-year-olds (Magic Johnson and Yo-Yo Ma); three baseball Hall of Famers (Ted Williams, Mickey Mantle, and Willie Mays); and a four-time Super Bowl–winning quarterback (Joe Montana).

I interviewed artists, sculptors, musicians, authors, adventurers, cowboys, and scientists. Also, busty Morganna the Kissing Bandit (she signed her Christmas card "Breast Wishes"), and Candy Loving, Playboy magazine's 25th-anniversary Playmate (clothes on, no makeup . . . both of us, actually).

I interviewed the first man to the top of Mount Everest (with Hilary), Sherpa Tenzing Norgay, and the first man to ski down Everest, Yuichiro Miura. I hung out by the pool with supermodels Marie Helvin and Jerry Hall. I might be the only journalist, dead or alive, to interview both actress Susan Saint James (birth name: Susan Jane Miller) and sex worker–activist Margo St. James (birth name: Margaret Jean St. James).

I traveled with a bluegrass band, was wrapped in a playful headlock by Muhammad Ali, had an elevator encounter with Jane Fonda, and got my tie straightened on a movie set by Janet Jackson.

I never thought of myself as a risk taker and didn't consider myself particularly restless. Yet when I moved to Atlanta in 1994, Georgia became the seventh state I had lived in since college. Along the way, I walked away from good jobs and bewildered employers, and blew a six-figure inheritance.

I failed at multiple relationships and was divorced twice. On my best days I was an inadequate father and grandfather to my daughters and grandchildren.

I was nominated for Pulitzer Prizes three times and didn't win. I won a national award for a magazine story but didn't get the grand prize. I was interviewed for a National Endowment for the Arts grant, and didn't get that either.

I was much like the prodigal son who squanders his wealth and finds himself feeding pigs. If someone had put a gun to my head, I would have confessed to feeling like a failure. It didn't seem likely that I'd wind up feeding pigs, but I couldn't foreclose on the possibility of sleeping under an overpass.

But one evening at CNN I got into a conversation with a security guard. He was a trim, well-spoken guy whom I guessed to be of Middle Eastern descent. I don't know how the conversation started or what we were discussing, but it must have had something to do with spirituality.

At one point, he smiled and said, "I'm a Baha'i, and you're what we call a seeker."

He was right. The things that others aspired to—money, possessions, prestige—didn't interest me. From the time I was young, I felt inadequate and unwelcome. Despite occasional successes and more than my fair share of redeeming qualities, I was always looking for something that would make me feel good about myself.

I didn't have a plan, but I did have hope. I went through life collecting experiences and broadening my perspective, but never finding the answer. Meanwhile, being employed and having a steady income had a certain insulating charm. I was still in the game, still looking, still hoping, still getting by.

When I was a kid, my father used to scold me for underachieving. "You're lazy," he would say. "You're drifting."

Rookie mistake by a first-time dad. I was the first of his five sons, and in that grainy, black-and-white era he thought I should do what he wanted me to do. I should be like him. I had my own ideas. What he thought was laziness was passive aggression, my only means of self-defense at the time. The drifting was a decoy, a false front for a real and intense need simply to feel better and be better.

I was still drifting and still searching in June 2000 when I drove to Appalachia to report on the manhunt. I figured I'd do some interviews and research, write a story, and move on.

I was wrong. What happened in the next 18 months would ultimately change my life.

Chapter 01

Bypassed

The four-lane highway that carries Routes 19, 74, and 129 through the far southwestern corner of North Carolina splits a long, wide valley that runs northeast to southwest. On either side of the valley are the heavily wooded peaks and ridges of the Smoky Mountains. When it rains, as it did on my first visit in June 2000, ribbons of mist rise from the forests like smoke from secret fires.

I was a senior writer for CNN.com and had gone to the Smokies to report on the largest manhunt in US history. The fugitive was a 32-year-old former paratrooper named Eric Robert Rudolph. Rudolph was suspected of setting off three bombs in Atlanta, Georgia, in 1996 and another in Birmingham, Alabama, in 1998, which killed two people and wounded 120 others. The targets were two abortion clinics, a lesbian bar, and the Olympic Games.

Rudolph was thought to be hiding in the Nantahala National Forest, an area in the Smokies where he had lived as a teenager. But two years of searching had not produced so much as a glimpse of Rudolph, and the task force had dwindled to six officers.

The search was centered in the town of Andrews, which is situated at the northeastern end of the valley, a half-mile off the four-lane highway. The center of town is a four-block stretch of buildings, mostly brick, that appear to rise out of pastures just a few blocks away. From a distance it looks like a movie set.

Before the four-lane was built—the locals, I would learn, called it "the four-lane," as if it were a living entity—the shortest route between Asheville, North Carolina, two hours to the northeast, and Chattanooga, Tennessee, two hours to the west, ran right through downtown Andrews.

Andrews was prosperous in those days. There were pharmacies, grocery stores, furniture stores, an appliance store, a theater, a Western Union office, clothiers, a post office, two hardware stores, and a feed and seed merchant. There were also, at various times, a lumber company, a tannery, and a railroad.

Fifty years later, a traveler could bypass Andrews without so much as a thought, and most did. A few buildings on Main Street appeared to be inhabited and in good repair when I drove into town, but there were empty storefronts on every block and only a few cars parked on the street.

The effect on a rainy day was gloomy and disappointing when I checked into the Bradley Inn, a modest, two-story brick structure on Main Street. The place was a former hotel that had been renovated and converted into a bed and breakfast. The ground floor was occupied on one side by a coffee and gift shop and on the other by a home decor business. The rooms were on the second floor.

"So, you're here to do a story about Rudolph," said innkeeper Jo Jones as she showed me my room, a Victorian romp down to knick-knacks and a doorstop.

"Well, come down in the morning and have coffee at Treats, the coffee shop," she said. "But I don't know if anyone will talk. A lot of people around here are pretty upset with the media. It seems like every time we turned on the TV, they'd be interviewing someone with no teeth and tobacco juice trickling out of his mouth, and people here were offended."

Bright June sunshine angled through the windows when I entered the coffee shop the next morning. The gift shop on the left featured displays of dishes, dolls, figurines, and porcelain angels. The coffee shop on the right included a few tables and chairs and a counter.

Mrs. Jones led me to a big table toward the back where four middle-aged men were sitting, and introduced me as a reporter from Atlanta. I didn't realize it at the time, but finding the coffee shop was a stroke of luck. From what I could tell, it was the only place in town where some of the town's citizens gathered regularly.

I sat down next to a slender, bespectacled man in his late 50s wearing black slacks, a black shirt, and a white clerical collar. He introduced himself as George Simmons, the pastor of St. Andrew Lutheran Church. Rev. Simmons had thinning white hair and a white beard, and sparkling blue eyes that hinted at mischief.

He poured cream into a glass mug of coffee and spooned homemade raspberry jam onto a bagel. Nodding at the jar of jam, he joked, "You don't want any of that. It's not any good."

Next to him was Tony Caivano, stocky, bearded, and easily the youngest of the group.

Across from Caivano was Scott Freel, a tall, rangy man with red hair and a goatee. Freel wore jeans, a golf shirt, and cowboy boots. Like Caivano, Freel was drinking peach tea, and I got the impression he was a businessman of some kind. I also recalled seeing a sign at the edge of town informing me that I was crossing the Margaret Walker Freel Bridge.

Next to Freel, in T-shirt, shorts, and a stained chef's apron, was Roy Peacock, the owner of a popular restaurant called Chestnuts Cafe.

After introductions—firm handshakes, polite smiles, cool appraisals—conversation returned to the sinking of Caivano's Jet Ski the previous weekend.

Caivano and friends had gone to a lake and borrowed a boat to go fishing. As they pulled away from shore, the motor died. When they were unable to restart it, the boat's owner, who was watching from shore, climbed aboard Caivano's Jet Ski and rode out to help.

But the man weighed nearly 400 pounds, and the rear of the Jet Ski sank so low that the engine compartment flooded. Each time he tried to restart the engine, more water was sucked into the engine, and finally Jet Ski and rider both sank.

Both were rescued, dragged back to shore, and drained of superfluous fluids. The Jet Ski was being repaired, and updates on its progress, I would discover, were a regular feature of coffee at Treats. There were no updates on the man.

Eventually Caivano turned to me. "You're here to do a story about Rudolph?"

I nodded, and a chill settled over the gathering. When I asked if anyone cared to be interviewed, only Rev. Simmons volunteered. When I pulled out a pad and pen, the others put money on the table and left.

Rev. Simmons tried to be helpful, but he had told his story so often it sounded rehearsed: the federal agents who had poured into town were dedicated professionals; some folks thought Rudolph was still around, some didn't; some thought he was a kind of Robin Hood, while others considered him an outlaw.

I asked if people were concerned that Rudolph was still at large.

"I don't think they see it as a threat," Rev. Simmons said. "They feel he didn't turn against the local people. His concern was abortion."

Based on where the bombs exploded, Rudolph's concern was also gays and lesbians. It later turned out that Rudolph also construed the Olympic Games as a disturbing form of "global socialism."

Considering that Rudolph, his mother, and siblings had lived thirteen miles away in Nantahala for many years, I asked Rev. Simmons what he said to his congregation about Rudolph.

"We prayed for Eric, for his family, and for the agents," he said. "We prayed for a peaceful resolution to the issue at hand."

He sipped his coffee. "Later, someone asked me, 'Why pray for Eric and his family?' I said the Lord of the church said we pray for all people in all situations."

After Rev. Simmons left, I stepped out into the sunlight and found that the town had a much different feel from the gloomy day before. If not transformed, it had at least a shy charm of its own, and I decided to go for a ride.

Just a block off Main Street there were modest homes with neatly trimmed lawns and large shade trees. There were small neighborhoods of mobile homes that had long since become permanent structures, many of them with additions, sheds, gardens, and swings in the yard.

There were a few big homes, and at least a couple of them appeared to be empty and needing maintenance. But on lots that would be lavish in a city, there were often simple, well-kept homes with neat, pleasant yards that bespoke a modest lifestyle. Andrews was not a place where people put on airs.

I drove up Cherry Street, past the white-frame Presbyterian church and its tall, leafy trees, and saw an elderly couple sitting in the shade. They didn't know me or my car, of course, but they waved as I passed, and I waved back.

A few blocks farther along, a young man in a pickup headed in the opposite direction lifted two fingers off the steering wheel in greeting as we passed each other. I waved back.

I also noticed something I had overlooked earlier.

From just about anywhere in Andrews, you can see the green, rugged foothills of the Smokies. Standing shoulder to shoulder in the north, east, and south, they neither crowd the town, nor are they far away. They are the backdrop of every moment and every day in Andrews, a comforting reminder of nature's beauty and majesty.

Chapter 02

Exodus

That afternoon, I walked two blocks up Main Street from the Bradley Inn to town hall, an odd, two-story stone structure with a single-story wing to the right that housed the police department.

I had come to see Mayor Jim Dailey, whose office was in a loft above the clerk's office. The stairway to the loft paused at a landing halfway up where a door led to the police department.

Dailey, 50, was a tall, easy-going man with a red mustache and hair and a soft, twanging drawl. He greeted me politely and invited me to sit down.

The walls were paneled in dark veneer, and the room was dominated by a large conference table. Dailey's desk was covered by a welter of papers, rolled-up plans, and a monthly calendar without an empty square on it. Hanging on the wall behind the desk were photographs of a snow-covered forest and an autographed picture of stock car driver Dale Earnhardt.

On the front corner of Dailey's desk was a trophy of two small bronze basketball shoes so outdated they must have been cast in the 1950s. On the trophy was an inscription: "Coach Jim Dailey. Thanks for the Memories. '97–'98 Andrews Wildcats."

The conference table was to one side of Dailey's desk, and seated at the far end was an older man with a white beard and hair and a scowl on his craggy face. Dailey made no effort to introduce him, and he neither introduced himself nor offered to leave.

My first thought was that civilities that are customary elsewhere might not be observed in Andrews. But the longer I sat there, the more it seemed that my unexpected visit had interrupted an argument.

Since my intention was to get a feel for the town and the context for the manhunt, whatever was going on between them was none of my business. I didn't expect to see either of them again anyway.

In any event, Dailey seemed to welcome the interruption and gladly talked about growing up in Andrews.

"When I was a kid, we lived in housing that was built for the tannery around the turn of the century," he said. "'Course, the tannery went out of business, and a lot of other things have, too. My wife worked at the VF plant near the four-lane. They used to make Lee jeans, but they left town, too."

He paused. "There used to be a Ford dealer right across the street from here, and the barber shop was open six days a week, instead of two. We had a taxi stand, a pool hall, and three small mom-and-pop groceries. It was a booming little town in the early '60s."

Before he became mayor, Dailey worked at the Goodyear tire store 14 miles down the four-lane in Murphy. Murphy, the seat of Cherokee County, had a population of 20,000 and was a frequent frame of reference in Andrews. If Andrews didn't have something—and very often it didn't—Murphy usually did.

As for attractions, Dailey admitted that Andrews didn't have many. There were no buildings of architectural repute, no theme parks, no golf courses, no monuments, no public gardens, no gorges, no waterfalls, nothing that would attract visitors in a region abloom with tourism.

A few handsome old homes had been renovated, but tourists didn't come to the area to see Andrews. They came to see Nantahala Gorge in Nantahala, Joyce Kilmer Memorial Forest near Robbinsville, or the casino in Cherokee.

Dailey shook his head. "I've got two teenage daughters from my wife's first marriage, and we've got a side business washing and detailing automobiles, but there's not much work around here."

Dailey said he'd been "looking to slow down and smell the roses" before he ran for office, but being mayor as well as the town's administrator and finance officer was more time-consuming and worrisome than he imagined.

I glanced at the other man. He was staring at Dailey, still scowling.

The problem, Dailey said, was that the economic boom of the 1990s had bypassed Andrews the way travelers bypass Andrews on the four-lane.

"Per capita income here in Cherokee County is only about $20,000, and it's even lower in Andrews," he said. "Jobs were already scarce, and when the Levi Strauss plant in Murphy closed, a lot of folks in Andrews lost their jobs.

"Then the Baker Furniture plant in Andrews shut down, and that put another 375 people out of work," he said. "We had a new Food Lion supermarket, but it only lasted a year before it closed, and the new Walmart in Murphy is taking business from local businesses."

A Hardee's fast-food restaurant and a Microtel were expected to open soon, he said, but nobody was stepping up to fill those empty storefronts on Main Street.

"It would be nice if people comin' to town didn't see that," he said, shaking his head. "But it's kinda tough. We need jobs in the county. The kids who go to college don't want to come back."

In 1990, Andrews had an all-time high of 2,551 residents. Ten years later, it was 1,602. A 37 percent drop in population is not a trend. It's an exodus.

On the other hand, Dailey admitted that the manhunt for Rudolph had been good for business.

"There were 50 satellite trucks down by the park, and the railroad depot was full," he said. "You couldn't hardly walk down the street without bein' asked to talk."

He shrugged. "The media was aggressive to a lot of people, but they had a job to do, too."

The federal law enforcement people, he said, were "good neighbors and good people. I hated to see 'em go."

As for Rudolph, he said, "He never comes up in everyday life. You don't hear that much about him. What he did was wrong, but I don't like what abortion clinics do. They're taking lives, too, and they don't have a choice, that little boy or girl. They're killing people, too, but I don't think you should bomb the place. I don't think you should take people's lives."

That brought to mind school shootings, gangs, and what Dailey saw as a trend elsewhere in the country. It was a development so "scary" that he used the word three times.

"I wouldn't like to be a young person growing up today," he said.

Dailey said he and his wife had built a new house recently, but it didn't seem to give him much pleasure. "I was happy in the old one," he said. "We'd been in it since '76. I didn't want to move, but my wife and kids did."

He was quiet for a moment, then looked up. "Now, though, I can sit on the porch and look out across the hills."

He smiled, almost apologetically.

"I've been to Atlanta and I know that's where the money is, but all that traffic. . . . I can get in the car here and in a few minutes I'm driving on country roads, seeing some of the most beautiful country. I couldn't leave this. This job don't pay much, but there's no way I could leave this."

Back at the Bradley Inn, I asked innkeeper Jo Jones where I could find Scott Freel.

"Freel Builders Supply," she said, "but he was pretty angry about the way Andrews was portrayed by the media. He said he would never talk to the media."

She told me that the Freels were the most prominent family in Andrews. Freel Builders Supply was one of the town's biggest businesses, and the bridge at the edge of town was named for Freel's mother. Mrs. Freel, I learned, was an English teacher at the high school as well as the county historian, and had written a book about Andrews.

Despite Mrs. Jones's warning, I wanted to talk to Freel. At coffee that morning he had seemed smart, easygoing, and thoughtful. Whatever his feelings about the media, I figured it was worth a try. He could always say no.

When I drove into the parking lot at Freel Builders Supply, Freel was on top of an enormous machine nearly seven feet high. He was bent over and tugging at something, but straightened up and stared at the car as I drove up.

"Hey," he said when I got out.

I couldn't read his expression, but he didn't seem unhappy to see me. He climbed down holding a piece of black rubber and held it out so I could see a long, jagged rip on one side of it.

"I've got no idea what that is," I said, "but looks like you need a new one."

"Man's got to do 'bout everything around here," he drawled. He seemed to be in a good mood and launched into a brief soliloquy on living in a small town and having to fix your own hay baler.

I told him I was looking for background information about Andrews for the manhunt story. Would he mind answering a few questions?

When he agreed, I asked who the major employers were in Andrews.

"Well, there's the hospital, the building industry, and the schools," he said. "But if you can make a living in Andrews, you're lucky. My neighbor drives 75 miles one way to Canton, Georgia, to work so he can live here. I have cows, horses, rental property and a building supply business so I can make a living."

He admitted that it wasn't easy to be optimistic about Andrews's future given the economic realities, but pointed out that some people had moved into town simply because it was peaceful.

"I'd like to see it stay the way it is," he said, "but my living depends on the opposite."

I asked him what the media had done that upset him.

"Eric Rudolph isn't even from here," he said, his face beginning to flush. Rudolph was born in Florida and moved to Nantahala when he was fifteen. "He came here from somewhere else. And the media makes it look like we're a bunch of people with no teeth, beat-up vehicles, Rebel flags on our barns, and antigovernment, too. We're not that way. . . . We may walk slow and talk slow, but we're not dumb.

"I don't care for abortion," he continued, "but I don't believe anyone should tell a woman what to do with her body. The majority of the people here are God-fearin', hard-workin' people who just want to live their lives."

We chatted a bit longer, but I'd gotten what I was looking for. I thanked Freel and left.

Chapter 03

Singer

The grill was broken at Reid's Place when I stopped there the next day for lunch. Every time a car pulled into the parking lot, Teresa Bateman hurried out into the settling dust, hands clutched in front of her, and said, "I'm sorry, my grill's broke and my husband's gone for parts, and I don't know when we'll have it workin'. I'm really sorry."

People expecting to have one of the hamburgers that were the restaurant's specialty swallowed their disappointment, thanked her, and said it was all right. They understood, and they hoped she got it fixed real soon. Some even lingered to chat with her through the car window, a custom that in just two days I had already noticed. No one, it seemed, was too busy to stop for a few minutes and visit.

Between trips to the parking lot, Mrs. Bateman sat on the roofed porch of her mobile-home-turned-restaurant and talked about the manhunt that had dragged Andrews into the international spotlight.

She had blonde hair, soulful brown eyes, and the watchful air of an older sister. She was also, I learned later, the lead singer of a country band that would just about have to be called Heartbreak. Word was she sounded like Tanya Tucker.

"Please call me Teresa," she said, hands in her lap. "I bought this place from my parents, Wanda and Clyde. There were eight of us kids in the family. My sister Sheila helps me run it."

She pointed at a man mowing the field next to the parking lot. "That's my brother, James," she said. (Twenty years later, visitors to the Andrews website would find a picture of James Reid identifying him as the mayor.)

Behind Teresa on the deck, lying next to a vending machine, were two small brown and white puppies. Heads between their paws, they watched the comings and goings with bewildered eyes.

"Somebody found 'em on the road," she said with a sigh. "'Course, they brought 'em here. I don't know what I'm supposed to do with 'em."

When Rudolph was traced to this area back in the fall of 1998, law enforcement people and the media descended on Andrews like a biblical plague. Motels, inns, and bed and breakfasts were filled to overflowing, forcing some to stay 20 or 30 miles away in North Georgia.

Restaurants were so busy that folks had to wait an hour and more, something unheard of in Andrews. Reporters and camera crews wandered through town looking for people who knew Rudolph, or knew someone who knew someone who knew Rudolph.

Local faces kept turning up on national TV, and as Freel and Mrs. Jones had before her, Teresa lamented that those man-in-the-street interviews didn't always reflect fairly on the town.

"Seems like they always showed the stupid people," she said. "I figured if I got on camera, I'd be one of 'em."

On the other hand, every day at the restaurant was like Christmas morning. Vans rolled into the parking lot at lunchtime filled with federal agents eager for one of its thick, juicy, cholesterol-inducing hamburgers.

"Lord, there were so many that the regular customers couldn't get in," she said, shaking her head. "It was hard feeding them all. But they were really nice. Never a word out of the way, very courteous. They gave me their business, they ate, and they left. I hated to see 'em all go."

An elderly man came around the corner and climbed the steps to the porch. He had pale, mottled skin and a halting gait. Teresa rose to greet him.

"Teresa," he said, holding out some folded bills, "I brought you that money I owed you."

"Oh, Daddy," she said, "you didn't have to do that. I don't need it. . . ."

She tucked the bills into her jeans and introduced me to Clyde Reid. We chatted briefly, but Mr. Reid had the air of a man whose mind was elsewhere, and after a few minutes he drifted away.

Teresa picked up a rag to wipe off a picnic table and the counter that ran along the front railing. One of the roof beams and the spindles on either side of it were dented, and I asked what happened.

"A woman's gas pedal stuck when she started her car and she hit the fence," Teresa said. "It made a terrible loud noise. I was inside cooking and I thought, Oh my God, they bombed me! They've seen all the FBI guys here, and they bombed me."

Chapter 04

Outsiders

Western North Carolina is isolated from the rest of the state by distance and topography, but also by sensibility. The people whom Teresa Bateman thought had bombed her restaurant were militia and antigovernment groups that lived in the area.

When the manhunt was at its peak, leaflets were distributed that complained about the presence of "jack-booted thugs" and asked "How long will we tolerate the presence of these brutal tyrants?"

The language had an absurd, comic-book ring to it, but apparently some people took it seriously. Not long after the manhunt began in November 1998, eight shots were fired into the task force's compound. One of the bullets grazed the skull of an FBI agent.

The culprit turned out to be a local man who had an assault rifle, too much to drink, and a whopping case of xenophobia. He was arrested, convicted, and sent to prison. Rudolph himself was said to have sympathies with a militant, racist, anti-Semitic group called Christian Identity, and a right-wing ideologue named Nord Davis.

Suspicion of strangers is hardly unique to Western North Carolina, of course, but nowhere in this country might there be better cause for it.

In the 1830s, gold was discovered in the area. The land was owned by the Cherokee Indians, and in one of the most infamous acts in American history, tribal leaders were induced to sign a treaty ceding all Cherokee lands east of the Mississippi River to the US government. The selling price for this enormous tract was $5 million.

The treaty was repudiated by a majority of the tribe members, and their rights were upheld by the US Supreme Court. But President Andrew Jackson and local officials refused to enforce the decision, and 15,000 people were forcibly removed and marched to Oklahoma.

On that 116-day journey known as the Trail of Tears, more than 4,000 Cherokee died.

In the decades that followed, many white settlers were also uprooted. The mountains are too rugged for large-scale farming or plantations, and there were few slaves in the area. As a result, the region was largely indifferent to the Civil War and became a haven for renegades and deserters from both sides.

But when logging, mining, and railroad companies moved in, they also removed families and devastated the land. When those industries left the area near the turn of the twentieth century, the ravaged landscape was turned over to the embryonic US Park and Forest Services and, later, the Tennessee Valley Authority.

The TVA not only forced people off their land, it also built dams and buried entire towns and valleys under water. The federal government is still the largest landholder in the area, but the fees it pays for use of the land are far less than what it would fetch from property taxes.

"There are very few regions where white people have been forcibly removed from their lands as they have been in southern Appalachia," said Curtis Wood, a professor of history at Western Carolina University. (Andrews is in the foothills of the Smoky Mountains. The Smokies are part of the Blue Ridge Mountains, which are part of the Appalachian Mountain range that stretches from central Alabama to Newfoundland, Canada.)

"The attitudes of southern mountain people toward the government have been shaped by their experiences," Wood said. "They've seen their land taken out of their control and put into big programs, leaving them with diminished resources and not much in return."

With this as a regional legacy, and perhaps mindful of federal involvement in sieges at Waco, Texas, and Ruby Ridge, Idaho, the people of Andrews held their breath when the manhunt began.

But there were no jack-booted thugs, no brutal tyrants. Instead, the federal agents turned their stay into a church social. They visited Cub Scout meetings, showing kids their night-vision goggles and bulletproof vests. They gave the kids badges and keychains.

Agents cut firewood for an elderly woman; she repaid them with fried chicken. Two agents drove three hours after work one evening to visit an Andrews woman who'd been hospitalized in Atlanta, then turned around and drove back.

Helicopter surveillance flights were rescheduled when a Baptist minister complained that they disrupted his Sunday evening services. Several agents looked in on the elderly mother of Jo Jones, the innkeeper, when she and her husband left town to attend a funeral.

Mrs. Jones told me she still got notes, emails and Christmas cards long after they left from agents who stayed at the inn. She also recalled fondly a Thanksgiving dinner at the inn that included a mix of local people and agents.

"There were 16 of us, and it went on from five in the afternoon to midnight," she said. "They talked for hours about their homes and their families and their communities. It really was a wonderful situation. They turned out to be wonderful, kind people."

I heard so many testimonials about the agents that when I got back to Atlanta I called the FBI in Washington. I wanted to know whether their behavior had been part of a carefully planned public relations offensive or was a genuine response to circumstances.

No one returned my call, but in my visits to Andrews I never once heard a complaint about the agents' behavior.

Chapter O5

Purgatory

The next day I drove over the ridge from Andrews to Nantahala, the area where Rudolph had lived for many years and where he was last seen. I drove east out of Andrews, then took Junaluska Road, which climbs to the ridge that separates Andrews and Nantahala, and Cherokee and Macon Counties as well.

Small houses, the forest, and the ridge itself pressed ever closer to the road as I climbed the ridge. It was beautiful in the sunshine, but the curtain of hardwoods, pines, and tangled undergrowth on both sides of the road was so dense that sunlight seldom reached the forest floor.

It was almost depressing, like something from a Stephen King novel.

During the height of the manhunt, I learned later, a small plane crashed in this wilderness. Although it was equipped with a homing beacon, searchers were unable to find it until they actually stood beneath the tree where it hung, nose down, like a sleeping bat.

"We've got satellites flying over that area that can read a license plate on a car," Patrick Crosby, a spokesman for the task force, told me. "But that forest is so thick you couldn't see a Chevy!"

It seemed to me that if Rudolph was, indeed, hiding in that forest, he was in a purgatory of his own making.

I turned onto Wayah Road in Nantahala and found my way to the Lake's End Grill, a rustic restaurant tucked among tall pines at the edge of Lake Nantahala. During the early days of the manhunt, the grill had put a message on its signboard that read "Rudolph Eats Here."

The grill, a single large room, was simple and unpretentious. The smell of cooking oil hung in the air, and a TV was tuned to a soap opera. The only customer was a man drinking coffee at a table against the back wall.

Meanwhile, a waitress was carrying cases of food from a cooler to a long counter.

I sat down at the counter and chatted with her as she worked. She was friendly and sociable until I told her I was a journalist doing a story about Rudolph.

"I mighta knowed," she said, scowling.

"What do folks around here think about him?" I asked.

"Nobody talks about him," she said, setting a case on the counter.

"Did you know any of his family?"

"I didn't know none o' them."

I asked where the town of Nantahala was. All I had seen was the restaurant, a few cottages, and a small store.

"This is about it," she said.

A half-mile or so beyond the restaurant I passed a small green pasture with an abandoned mobile home in it. One side of the structure had collapsed, spilling the contents—including a white porcelain toilet—into the field. The building was so old and so far gone to ruin that it almost transcended squalor and acquired a kind of historical fascination, an archaeological find without the digging.

I drove on, following the twisting, heavily wooded shore of Lake Nantahala for perhaps a mile. I'd been told that the lake, which is man-made, is the clearest and coldest in North Carolina.

On a midweek afternoon in June, it must also have been the loneliest. I didn't see a soul. No one boating, water-skiing, kayaking, or canoeing. No one fishing—on the lake or from the shore. No one even sitting on the shore, soaking in the pastoral calm.

Driving back up Wayah Road, I passed a farm where chickens and goats wandered amid cars and trucks that appeared to have been abandoned where they gave out. I wanted to be disgusted at the chaos and clutter but couldn't, perhaps because weeds, wildflowers, and creatures had already begun to reclaim the place.

But I was less forgiving further up the road. A double-wide mobile home was perched on a low hill that had been scalped and leveled by a bulldozer. The soil was a gash of clay so red and raw one could almost believe it was in pain.

I turned up Junaluska Road and headed back to Andrews.

Chapter 06

Loner

It was mid-afternoon as I returned from Nantahala and descended Junaluska Road where it twists and winds down from the top of the ridge. At one point, the forest on one side and a ridge on the other pinched the road so tightly that the front porch of a small house was no more than 10 feet from the road.

Ten yards beyond the house, the road turned left and narrowed to one lane to cross a small bridge.

Glancing over the fence to my left, I saw a man sitting in a garden. He wore shorts and a battered fishing hat, but he was shirtless and his chest was as brown as mahogany. His eyes were closed, and he sat in a shaft of golden sunlight filtering down through the trees. On his face was a look of pure contentment. He looked like the happiest man in the world.

I crossed the bridge, parked on the side of the road, and walked back with my camera. That was a picture of pure bliss, and I wanted it on film.

But as I neared the fence, he opened his eyes and saw me. He waved, and I waved back.

"Okay if I take your picture?" I asked.

He cupped his hand behind his ear.

"Can I take your picture?" I shouted. I held up the camera. He smiled and nodded, and I snapped a couple of shots, but it wasn't the same. The spell was broken when saw me.

He got up and beckoned to me. "Hey, c'mere," he said. "I want to show you somethin'."

I followed the fence around to the dirt driveway and the house I had just driven past. The house was old and looked like it needed repairs, or maybe just a coat of paint. An old, two-toned green Chevy Malibu was parked in a carport. An even older pickup truck, small, gray, and heavily oxidized, was parked in the driveway.

A battered old TV rested on a tree stump near the porch, its screen shattered. Lying among the pieces of broken glass on the ground were two spent red shotgun shells. My first thought was how often I had fantasized about shooting at something on TV, and here was somebody who'd done it. Then it occurred to me that although he seemed pleasant enough, this guy might be a nut.

He stepped onto the porch, bent over a small bookcase, and pulled out three reddish brown rocks. Each was a different size, but all three were cube-shaped, their edges rounded and smooth as if they'd been machined rather than shaped by nature.

"You ever see anything like this before?" he said. He was tall and had a potbelly, but his face was open and guileless, dark eyes alive with wonder.

"No," I said. "I never have."

"I never have either," he said. His voice had a whimsical, singsong quality that reminded me of Gomer Pyle. "You just don't see rocks like this," he said. "I found them in the woods."

He paused, as if revisiting the experience. "I think the Indians did it."

He narrowed his eyes and peered intently at me. "You know," he said, lowering his voice, "I think there's a lot we don't know about these mountains."

"I don't know anything about these mountains," I said, "but it wouldn't surprise me."

He told me his name was Bob McClure. I introduced myself and told him why I was in town.

"Do you want to see my garden?" he said.

"Sure."

It was an eccentric affair, with sunflowers in the middle, stalks of corn here and there, as if planted on a whim, along with tomato plants and other things I didn't recognize.

At the bottom of the garden, where the property was bordered on one side by the road and on the other by a creek, was a pond. It was perhaps twelve feet long, six or eight feet wide, and maybe three feet deep. On the near side there was a small wooden deck just big enough to accommodate a chair.

Swimming languidly in the pond were three fish about 10 or 12 inches long.

A few feet from the pond was the faded green chair he had been sitting in when I spotted him. There was another chair a few feet away, and in it was a box of bright red shotgun shells. Leaning against the chair was a glittering, black-barreled shotgun, cold and alien in this lush green landscape.

McClure saw me eyeing the gun. "I been tryin' to shoot a snake," he said. "He's eatin' my fish."

He gestured toward a shed behind him where the skin of a large raccoon was tacked to the wall. "He was eatin' 'em, too, but he got greedy," McClure said. "I don't like to kill things, but they were wiping me out."

McClure said he dug the pond several years before after the garden flooded and he found a 12-inch trout swimming in it. "I figured, well, the Great Spirit started it, I'll finish it."

I asked him where the fish came from.

"The stream," he said. "I catch 'em and put 'em in here, and then I eat 'em."

He smelled faintly of sweat and something I couldn't place at first. Then I saw a bottle of Miller High Life on the ground next to his chair.

He nodded at the bottle. "I drink three of 'em every night," he said. "Just seems to set me right for dinner."

There was a book lying in the chair where he'd been sitting, old and much used from the look of it.

"What're you reading?"

He held it up: Marcus Aurelius's *Meditations*. On a shelf below the raccoon skin were two more books—Modern Library editions of works by Plato and Aristotle.

McClure said he'd been reading Aristotle's views on the nature of reality, and it reminded him of something that happened years before.

"I'd been awake for four days," he said, "and all of a sudden I was way up in the air. I could see my body below, but I went in the other direction. The sky was bluer than blue, and there was a brilliant white light. I went into that light and I knew we were part of that light, that we are all light. And we are all one with the Creator."

He stopped, beaming, and crossed his arms on his chest.

I told him I knew a woman who had an out-of-body experience similar to his.

"She said she saw her body below on a gurney in the emergency room of the hospital," I said. "Then she saw brilliant light and tremendous beauty. She said she felt such peace that she wanted to keep going. But then she heard her son calling her, and she wound up back in her body."

He nodded.

"It's the most beautiful thing," he said, eyes alight. "I can't describe it, but since then I've felt like I'm being watched over. I go into the woods by myself, but I've always been okay. I've stepped over rattlesnakes in the woods and not been bit. Another time, I was fussin' with my woman—she was a good woman, but I'll tell you, she liked to fight too much. I just couldn't do it, you know what I mean?

"So I decided to go hunting. I got a few miles away and realized I forgot something, and went back to get it. When I got here, she came out of the house with a shotgun and she said, 'Get down on your knees, Bob McClure. I'm gonna blow you away.'

"But I didn't. I just kept walking at her, and when I got close enough, I grabbed the barrel of the gun and wrestled it away from her. Worst thing was, my little girl saw it all. I hated that. But I coulda gone then, too. I feel like my life has been a gift."

The marriage ended in a divorce, he said, just like the one before, and now he lived alone and liked it that way.

"But I'm glad you stopped," he said. "I'm pretty much a loner. I don't talk to people much, but I believe you can tell about people, don't you? And I had a good feeling about you."

Chapter 07

Wayah Bald

Three days in Andrews had provided me with all the information I needed for the Rudolph story, and it was time to go back to Atlanta. Rather than taking the most direct route that Friday afternoon, I drove east out of Andrews through Nantahala to Wayah Bald.

I had heard of various "balds" in North Georgia and North Carolina, and wanted to see one. At 5,385 feet, Wayah Bald is the highest point in that part of the Nantahala National Forest and was a popular hiking spot on the Appalachian Trail.

The forest is enormous. It covers more than 530,000 acres, and I had to follow Highways 1505, 1401, and 1310 through the same densely wooded landscape that prompted my rumination about Rudolph's private hell. Later

I learned that Nantahala is the Cherokee word for "land of the noonday sun," a reference to the sun reaching the forest floor only when it's directly overhead.

A dusty gravel road made a long, winding climb through the forest to a parking lot. A dirt path led from the parking lot to the overlook but was paved with fieldstone when it reached the overlook.

The first thing I noticed was not the view, but a two-story lookout tower to the left and well back from the lookout. It, too, was built from fieldstone.

The overlook itself was a wide area also paved with fieldstone and bordered by a low stone wall. The absence of trees—hence the "bald"—allowed for spectacular views in every direction. An endless procession of ridges and bowls extended as far as I could see, and everything was carpeted with thick green forest.

On a bright, somewhat hazy afternoon the visibility must have been twenty-five or thirty miles in the smudged air that gives the Smokies their name.

Below and well off to the right, wings wide, a hawk rode a thermal updraft rising up the face of the mountain. When I first spotted it, it was below me, but it climbed higher and higher in wide, effortless, clockwise circles.

At an altitude not much higher than I was, it suddenly folded its wings, shaping itself into a sharp, black wedge, and dropped like an anvil. Its speed was shocking, and I cringed as I watched, expecting to see an explosion of feathers when it struck some hapless bird.

But I lost sight of it when it dropped below the tree line, and I was grateful to be spared the violence in what was an otherwise serene and inspiring view.

Hearing a noise, I turned to see a hiker with a large backpack coming up the trail. He was lean and blond, and something about his appearance and gear made me think he was European—German, perhaps, or Austrian.

He dropped his pack, sat down on the ground, and took off his boots and socks. He pulled a paperback out of his pack, stretched out on his back, and propped his feet against the wall.

I turned back to the view.

A faint breeze played in the trees below. The sun was high and the air was warm. The birds and crickets were still. The only sound was the low, lazy muttering of a small airplane too far away to be seen,

As I turned to leave, I glanced over at the hiker. He was asleep, the opened book face down on his chest.

Chapter 08

Connections

I returned to Andrews the following month, but this time with a different objective. I had written and filed the Rudolph story, but I was fascinated by my experiences in Andrews and had to go back.

Initially I thought I was attracted to the local people's resentment at their treatment by the media, but it went beyond that. It was a way of life that seemed to be at stake. Here was a town that appeared to be dying, and yet in its people there was an orderliness and a calm that seemed to defy reality.

There was something in those 1.6 square miles that was missing from city life. It reminded me of other small towns I'd been, places where everyone seemed to belong and everyone was connected.

In the few days I had spent there, the people I had met were friendly and agreeable, and it seemed at odds with the economic situation. I would have expected them to be anxious and fretful, but I saw none of that.

That was the mystery I wanted to solve: why were these people so content?

But there was another reason I felt so drawn to the place, and frankly I didn't understand it at the time. That was the comfort I felt every morning when I had coffee with the regulars at Treats. I didn't realize how important it was to me personally that in just a few days, I felt like one of the regulars.

I looked forward to George Simmons joking about hoarding the jam. Tony Caivano would give an update on his Jet Ski. Scott Freel would mention something that happened at his business. Roy Peacock would announce that shredded pork barbecue was the lunch special at Chestnuts Cafe.

I didn't have to say much—or anything, for that matter. I just had to show up and participate in the ritual. Obviously my presence had caused a subtle shift in the dynamics of the group, but at the time it didn't seem that important. My focus was on everything but myself.

But before I went back, I called Jane Brown, an instructor in anthropology and history at Western Carolina University in Cullowhee. I told her that I was baffled. There was something going on in Andrews that

I didn't understand: a mindset, a way of being, an attitude toward life—something I couldn't quite grasp.

"It all has to do with the sense of place," she said. "You need to experience it. Otherwise, you can't relate to the things they say or what Appalachian life is like. It has something to do with the mountains."

The first call I made when I got back to Andrews was to Teresa Bateman.

When I interviewed her the first time, I had asked about the search for Rudolph and its impact on her business. But this time I wanted to ask her about growing up in Andrews, about her life with seven siblings and how it had changed, and what her hopes and expectations might be.

But when she answered the phone, she was tense and anxious.

"We just heard that my dad's been in an accident," she said. "He was comin' back from the doctor in Bryson City. We don't have any details yet. We're waitin' for someone to call."

When I got back to the Bradley Inn later that day, Jo Jones was at the front desk. We exchanged greetings, and she said, "Bad news. Clyde Reid was killed in an accident."

I stared at her, trying to make sense of it. It was as if she was speaking Urdu. I heard the words, but they didn't make any sense. I wasn't sure how she even knew that I had met Mr. Reid, but that was beside the point. The fact that he was dead was incomprehensible.

I had just met him a month earlier. I had shaken his hand. I had looked into his eyes. I had spoken with him. We had connected—tenuously, perhaps—but we had connected, and now that connection was broken.

I went up to my room and sat on the bed. I didn't even turn on the light.

I had come back to Andrews buoyed by the idea of collecting information for a story about the town and its people. I needed details to help me understand the "sense of place" that Jane Brown talked about.

For most of my career, my work involved sitting with a person or people for an hour or two, asking questions, and taking notes. The stories I wrote were essentially snapshots of those people taken in the moment.

In 1979 I interviewed marine biologist Dr. Sylvia Earle in the middle of the Pacific Ocean immediately after she set a world record for walking on the ocean floor 1,250 feet below. She was remarkably calm. The only outward signs that she had done anything more than go for a boat ride was her sweat-streaked face and how the diving helmet had plastered her hair to her forehead.

The next day I wrote 1,500 words about an extraordinary woman's courageous feat and gave it to my editor. End of story.

Clyde Reid's death was the first indication that something had changed. It had never occurred to me that the story I wanted to write, the mystery I wanted to solve, might include a death. Nor could I have imagined how strongly it would affect me.

Sitting in the darkened room, I kept trying to make sense of the loss I felt. I didn't know Mr. Reid well enough to mourn him as I would a friend, but losing that connection was disturbing—almost painful.

I wish I could say I understood what was happening at the time, but I did not. I was still the journalist, still the outsider, still focused on what was going on around me. I had no idea that a shift was taking place and that my role had changed.

I had come back to Andrew not to record an hour or two, but rather to document everyday experiences for days at a time. In effect, my assignment had become life in real time, and life in real time isn't a photograph. My confusion about Mr. Reid's death was that I still thought I was working on a snapshot when in reality it was a movie, and I had become one of the actors.

After dinner that evening, I wasn't ready to go back to my room, so I went for a ride. I drove past Reid's Place, which was closed, but hanging on the door was a plastic wreath of ivy, ferns, and white roses.

I drove out of town on Fairview Road headed roughly southwest and turned onto Pisgah Road, which runs south between two long ridges. It had been raining most of the day, and the sky was heavy with clouds. High up on the ridge to the right, a long streamer of wet, gray clouds hung like a tattered banner.

I passed modest, well-kept homes and small pastures that sloped up toward the mountains. In some places, smaller ridges worked their way down toward the valley, creating pocket versions of the "hollers" of Appalachian lore.

About a mile up the road, the rustic serenity was broken by a cluster of dingy mobile homes, sheds, and garages. Junked cars, tools, and agricultural oddments lay in the weeds and underbrush, as if someone had been cleaning out a barn and forgot to finish the job. A mood of sullen neglect hung over the place.

Beyond, however, the countryside was green and lush, even in the gathering gloom. After another half-mile or so, I pulled off onto a gravel side road and turned around. I coasted back down the grade, steered over to the shoulder on the left for no particular reason, and stopped twenty yards from the paved road.

There were empty fields on both sides of the gravel. Beyond the paved road another field sloped up past a low shed and a weathered gray barn to a thick stand of trees. Mist dangled in the air like Spanish moss.

I rolled down my window. There was nothing to do or see, particularly, and I had no clear idea why I was there. I was just . . . there.

In Atlanta, I live two miles from a general aviation airport, 500 yards as the crow flies from commuter and Amtrak rail lines, three blocks from a fire station, and two blocks from the busiest street in the city. The soundtrack is planes, trains, automobiles, and emergency vehicles every day, all day, and often at night as well.

Here it was . . . still. Quiet. Peaceful. I took a deep breath and exhaled. Nothing. I was listening to nothing.

Exhale again. Nothing.

Then, from the field across the road, drifted the lazy call of a bird: "Whee-to-whee."

Silence. Splat—a raindrop on the roof. Splat—another on the windshield.

Silence.

"Whee-to-whee."

Silence. Splat.

I closed my eyes and took a deep breath. With the exhale, the tension in my neck and shoulders released, the pressure of city life floating off into the mist. I slipped away from the ordinary and commonplace and into a reverie. Not quite here, not yet there.

And in that curiously expanded state I thought I heard something. It sounded like someone breathing, which of course was not possible. There was no one around.

I caught myself leaning forward slightly, straining.

There!

From the very edge of awareness, the faintest of sounds, a whispering, feathery sigh: "Ehhhhhhhhhhhh."

I shook my head to reassure myself that I wasn't imagining something.

Silence.

"Ehhhhhhhhhhhh."

It was not my imagination. And if it was not my imagination, the only thing that might produce such a sound was somewhere and everywhere around me—green and wet, solid, unmoving, mundane soil. Dirt. Earth itself.

Existential dilemma: If what I just experienced was true—and I had no doubt that it was—who could I tell? How could I explain in mere words the sensation? The amazement? The wonder?

Thoughts clamor for attention: scientists know that plants communicate with each other. Native Americans honor "Mother Earth": they call trees "the Standing People." Jimmy Buffett sang about "Mother Ocean."

I feel like I've been given a gift, and I want to share it. I want to share the wholeness of that feeling . . . being part of something so vast and so reassuring, something almost unimaginable. Actually, I'd like to go door-to-door and tell everyone, especially people without hope, people in pain, people in despair.

But the conventions of a lifetime fight back: I am a product of my environment—an urban environment. I am also—in this environment and others—an outsider. I am sitting alone in a car, parked on the wrong side of the road in the middle of nowhere with my windows open.

I feel exposed. I imagine someone driving past and seeing this fool sitting in the middle of nowhere with his windows open.

I turn the ignition key. The engine responds. Windshield wipers surge and whine. I drive back to town.

Chapter 09

New Yorker

The regulars were in the coffee shop when I arrived the next morning: George Simmons, Tony Caivano, Scott Freel, and Roy Peacock. They had been joined by Ray Rowles, a big, heavyset former Rhode Islander who had retired from the insurance business in Sarasota.

Conversation touched briefly on Peacock's separation from his wife. It looked like divorce, he said, looking rueful and resigned. No one could think of anything to say about that, so they moved on to the case of country singer Tim McGraw.

The question: should McGraw have taken a joyride on a policeman's horse last month? The general feeling was that it was just a prank, nothing serious.

But Caivano—the youngest by at least a decade and probably the most conservative in the group—took a law-and-order position. "Well, if that's okay," he said, "then I guess it's okay if I get into a police cruiser and take it for a ride."

Bad analogy. Everybody knew the few policemen in town. Instead of arguing right and wrong, they debated which of the officers would be least likely to be offended if someone took his cruiser around the block.

Not being familiar with the McGraw episode, I looked it up later, and it turned out that McGraw didn't ride the horse at all. That was another country singer, Kenny Chesney, at a concert in Buffalo, New York.

McGraw interfered with the deputies who were trying stop Chesney.

But facts were often early casualties in this group, and they weren't necessarily that important. What did matter was being there and keeping alive a fraternal, arms-length intimacy that added a special dimension to their lives.

After coffee, I drove out to interview Caivano at his office.

On my first visit to Andrews, he showed no interest in discussing the search for Rudolph. But when he learned that I had come back specifically to focus on Andrews, he had readily agreed to talk with me.

Caivano owned Creative Sportswear, which applied custom embroidery to hats, T-shirts, athletic bags, and other leisure gear. It was housed in a gleaming-white, one-story building about half a mile from downtown. Large plate-glass windows fronted a showroom with black-and-white checkerboard flooring and racks of gear bearing the company's handiwork.

Caivano's desk occupied a back corner of the room, and when I visited him there was nothing on it but a telephone. A glass cabinet held a collection of plastic cups, suntan lotion, and other promotional items. On the floor by his desk were a gym bag and a pair of sport shoes.

"I spend most of my time over there with my assistant," he said, nodding toward a large horizontal window. In the room beyond I could see three employees and a row of machines.

"What are those machines?" I asked.

"I've got three computers in there," he said, "but what you can see from here are the embroidering machines. They were made in Japan."

Caivano was 17 and had just finished his junior year of high school when his family moved to Andrews from the Bronx in New York City. He had never imagined leaving New York, which was the center of the universe as far as he was concerned, and he spent his senior year at Andrews High School in an uncomprehending daze.

"It was culture shock," he said. "I fought it the whole year. I went to school and I went home."

After graduation, he got a job driving a truck for Coca-Cola and worked his way up to area manager. When he was 23, he met Jerry Cox, the owner of Creative Sportswear.

"Jerry was looking to sell the business, and I wanted to own one," he said. "I also wanted to stay in Andrews, but I didn't want to depend on the local economy. When I realized that Jerry had clients all over the country, we made a deal."

He added, "We did it all verbally, on a handshake."

Business was good; life was good.

At 31, he owned a late-model Acura, a new Chevrolet pickup, and a Jet Ski. Eventually, he said, he would build a home in or near Andrews, but for the time being he lived 11 miles away in a mobile home near the town of Marble (population 300).

"I believe how much you enjoy your life is up to you," he said.

"But what would keep a New Yorker in a place like Andrews?" I asked.

"It's small enough to feel comfortable," he said. "Where I came from, if the light turns green, people are gunning their engines and honking at you. Not here. I know everybody and I speak to everybody. I don't know them intimately, but I speak to all of 'em. I'm on a first-name basis with the mayor. I see him about three times a week, and I couldn't say the same about Ed Koch or Dave Dinkins."

I told Caivano that I was standing outside the Bradley Inn earlier that morning when Mayor Jim Dailey drove by in a small white pickup. Dailey waved to me, and I waved back.

He nodded. "That's the way it is here. Everybody knows everybody."

"I've moved several times and often felt like an outsider," I said. "Since you're from New York, do you feel like the people here have accepted you?"

"Occasionally someone jokes that I'm not from here, but it's not a big deal," he said. "Newcomers have to open their arms before others are going to let them in."

He glanced down at the gym bag near his feet. It reminded him of a time he was out on his Jet Ski on Lake Nantahala.

"I turned off the motor and you could hear the wind coming through the trees," he said. "Then it came across the water and there was a rippling sound. Then I heard a splash, and looked up. It was about 100 feet away, a fish. In New York, there's so much noise from ambulances, cars, buses, trucks, horns, and all that people don't know what silence is. Here, if we stop talking, what do you hear?"

He stopped. The only sounds were the low hum of the air conditioning and the ticking of the clock on the wall.

He continued. "I was talking to a buddy in New York on the phone, and he said, 'I don't see how you can stay down there in the country.'"

Caivano chuckled. "They just don't know," he said. "I don't even want to go back there to visit. If people in New York ever got away even for a little while to visit, New York would be empty."

Finally I asked him, "Is there a downside to living in Andrews?"

"I do miss good Italian food," he said. "You can't get good pizza here. But I still wouldn't trade all the pizza in Brooklyn for Andrews."

Chapter 10

Native Son

Late that morning, I drove over to Freel Builders Supply. Like Caivano, Scott Freel had welcomed the news that I was back to write about Andrews, and invited me to his office.

I found him in a paneled room at the back of his showroom. He was in a high-backed leather chair working on a laptop. Sliding glass doors separated the office from the showroom, and when I knocked he gestured for me to come in and sit on a plaid couch against a side wall.

Like many tall men—he was six-foot-four—Freel stooped slightly to bring himself closer to a world that was not fashioned with him in mind. He had an unhurried drawl that turned "vehicle" into "VEE hick-el" and an easygoing sociability.

But he had his values on straight, and he wanted to know how I wore mine. Before I could begin the interview, he questioned me.

"Where are you from?"

"Michigan originally, but I moved a lot after that."

"Are you married?"

"No. Two divorces. Three if you count the eleven-year relationship between marriages."

"Got any kids?"

"Two daughters, three grandchildren."

"Where are they?"

"Charlotte and Boston."

"What do they do?"

"One's a chiropractor, the other's in the financial world."

"You go to church?"

"I do."

"So you believe in God?"

"I do."

When he had satisfied his curiosity—and he seemed particularly gratified that I had spiritual values—the interview began.

It turned out that Freel was not only a native son, but the town owed its very existence to a Freel.

In 1890 Freel's great-grandfather, a state senator, persuaded the Richmond and Danville Railroad to extend its line from Bryson City, North Carolina, to what was then called Valleytown. But rather than ending the line in Valleytown where the senator was a major landholder, the railroad's owners extended it a mile past the town.

They built a depot there and named it after one of the line's vice presidents, Colonel A. B. Andrews. The town of Andrews grew up around the depot and eventually eclipsed Valleytown.

"When I was growing up, I rode my bicycle every morning to my father's furniture store and swept out the place," Freel said. "When I was older and I wanted to see girls after school, I'd ride my bike to work, then walk to school, and my father would take the bike home at lunch."

Freel said his father never gave him an allowance. "But if my school lunch was $1.50, he'd pay me $3," Free said. "I had to be responsible for everything I went and did, but I always had the opportunity to make it, and he always paid me more than I was worth."

On a school trip to Washington, DC, Freel's classmates bought the usual souvenirs, but Freel didn't buy a thing. When his parents asked why, he said, "Shoot, I can buy 'bout anything I want cheaper here."

He fiddled with a pen for a moment and looked up. "I lived a sheltered life growing up," he said. "I could do anything I wanted to do."

Like his parents, Freel attended Western Carolina University in Cullowhee, which is less than 40 miles from Andrews. After graduating, he taught school for a year and then went into the insurance business.

He married, had a son, divorced, and remarried. His son was a student at the University of Virginia. "I tell him the same thing every time we talk or I write him a letter," Freel said. "I say, 'Never be afraid to be different. Anyone can go along with the crowd.'"

In 1992 Freel learned that the owner of the builders supply business was planning to close it. He and his father bought it, and Freel had been running it since. "I also build an occasional spec house on the side," he said.

A young guy in work clothes appeared in the doorway. "Scott," he said, "how much I owe you for that paint?"

Freel gazed blankly at him and leaned so far forward that his chin was inches from the desk. "I don't know," he said slowly. "Haven't figured it out yet."

"Well, you let me know, okay?"

"Don't worry about it."

When he left, Freel said, "Let's get something to eat."

We rode the few blocks to Roy Peacock's Chestnuts Café in Freel's black Suburban. There was a trailer hitch on the back of the Suburban and on it a decal that said "BAMA." The North Carolina license plate said "XLENCE." Both were references to the University of Alabama's football program.

Not only was Freel an admirer of Alabama football, his second wife, Margaret, was from Alabama. That Margaret Freel, however, was not the Margaret Walker Freel whose name I saw on a bridge at the outskirts of town. Margaret Walker Freel was Freel's mother, and I spoke briefly on the phone with her one afternoon. Her diction was pitch-perfect, and knowing that she had been an English teacher I imagined that she set the bar high for the kids at Andrews High School.

Caivano joined us at the restaurant, and when a waitress came to the table, Freel said to her, "Your ear any better?"

"It is," she said, and began to explain that there were three bones in the ear. "The hammer, the anvil, and—." She groped for the third.

"The stirrup," Freel said.

"That's it!" she said with a relieved smile.

After she left, I told Freel I was impressed that he knew about the waitress's health issues and the parts of the ear as well. "Everybody here knows everybody's business," he said, "and what they don't know sometimes they make up."

"Yeah, but you're never very far from a friend," Caivano said. "If you have a flat tire, there's always someone who'll help you."

Freel nodded. "If you fuss at your brother, it's okay," he said slowly, with "fuss" meaning "argue." "But if I do it, you're gonna take up for him. That's the way it is here. We go on, but if one of us needs help, he doesn't realize how many friends he has. This is a small town, but it's more like family. We cuss each other, but we help each other too."

He paused and looked out the window. A white pickup truck with a horse trailer hitched behind it was parked on the street, and a guy was painting something on the tailgate of the trailer.

"That's Dave Bristol," Freel said. "Used to be in the big leagues."

"The guy who managed the Cincinnati Reds?" I said.

He nodded. "One of my favorite people."

Just then, Bristol stepped back to survey his handiwork. A foot below where a motorist would see the rear ends of two horses, Bristol had painted in large, bright-red letters, "Don't Be What You See."

Chapter 11

Troubled Man

After lunch, I rode with Freel back to his business to get my car and then drove the few blocks to town hall.

It seemed like a good time to talk with Mayor Jim Dailey, and this time he was alone in his loft. As before, his desk was cluttered with papers and a plastic water bottle, and he was also covering for the clerk downstairs while she was at lunch.

Dailey was pleased to know that I was working on a story about Andrews this time and began to reminisce about how full of hope and promise the town had seemed when he was young. I had heard pretty much the same comments in my first visit, so I asked him what he thought could be done to fill some of the empty storefronts.

"Well, businesses that are interested in moving here change their mind when they find out there aren't any good roads for trucks coming from the south," he said. "I don't know what it takes to get the downtown going, but people make the town unique. The majority care for one another and help each other in their time of need, but sometimes it takes a tragedy. . . ."

His voice trailed off. He stopped, thought for a moment, and started again.

"You might not know you need a good friend, but they'll be there for you," he said. "If you care about one another, somewhere, somehow, somebody will come through and help you."

I'd just heard the same sentiment at lunch with Freel and Caivano, and I wondered if it was the town's unofficial slogan: "Come to Andrews! We've got your back!"

It wasn't that I doubted that it was true, but Dailey's comment about tragedy struck me as odd. I was expecting a public relations pitch, something optimistic and hopeful, something that might make readers think that Andrews was the land of opportunity.

Instead, he seemed distracted and even a little depressed. I had no idea whether it was personal or had something to do with the job. I didn't want to press him, but I didn't want to ignore it either.

So I asked him, "Is being mayor about what you expected it to be?"

"Of course, everybody knows your business, good and bad," he said. "I'm watched every day, and there are rumors about me. Some people just look for the negative. As mayor, I'm accused of things, and no one comes to talk to me about them. I've caught a lot of static. I've got to decide if I want to do this again."

He stared at his desk for a moment, then looked at me.

"You know," he said, "sometimes I thought my brother would go into politics. To me, politics is crooked. I'm doing the best I can, but people talk and there's no way I can please everyone."

Hearing the door to the clerk's office open below, he got up, went over to the railing, and called out, "She'll be right back."

"Oh, that's all right," said a woman, sounding startled. "I thought there was nobody here."

"No, no," he said. "She'll be right there."

When he sat down, I said, "Why did you run for mayor?"

He shrugged. "It's hard to find people who'll do it," he said, "and I enjoy it at times. You have good days and bad days. But it's been tough on my wife and kids."

This was difficult terrain. I was there as a journalist to talk about Andrews and why people were so attached to the place. My hope was that Dailey as mayor could help me understand the people and their attachment.

Instead, it seemed as if I had happened upon an open wound. I wondered if instead of talking to a journalist with a pad and pen, perhaps Dailey should be talking to a therapist.

To change the subject, I mentioned that the newcomers I'd met seemed to appreciate Andrews more than some local people.

"That's true," he said. "It's like life—you take the familiar for granted. You assume you're going to be here. The beauty is what draws people, or this would be a ghost town. And the locals are learning to accept them. A lot of the people moving in are good people."

But Dailey couldn't help being nostalgic for the old days.

"You could go to a restaurant and get pinto beans, cornbread, and biscuits and gravy," he said with a wistful smile. "A good ol' country meal."

That was about as much optimism as Dailey could muster, so I thanked him for his time and left. Walking back to the Bradley Inn in brilliant July sunshine, I felt sorry for Dailey. He was a quiet, soft-spoken guy, and obviously troubled. I wondered if he was just too thin-skinned for politics.

But in a few months, he was going to prove himself right, because nobody in Andrews would need friendship and goodwill more than Jim Dailey.

That evening I decided to go for another ride.

It being July, the early evening sun was still high in the west as I drove to the foot of Schoolhouse Hill, a long, grassy slope just a block off Main Street. I stopped at an intersection and waited as a middle-aged guy on an old cruiser bicycle pedaled slowly through from left to right.

He wore jeans, a black T-shirt bearing the words "No Sweat," and a faded Atlanta Braves baseball cap. Cradled in his left arm was a dozing toddler in a T-shirt and diaper, his blond head resting on the man's shoulder.

I turned and followed slowly as he pedaled down the center of the empty street, the lush canopy of leaves overhead awash in golden sunlight. When I drew abreast of him, I said through my open window, "Never seen a baby put to sleep that way before."

He looked over at me and grinned, gaps showing where his front teeth were missing, and said in a deep drawl, "Works ever' time."

Chapter 12

Hick from Ohio

After coffee with the regulars the next morning, I drove through town and stopped at a produce stand across from the Alcoholic Beverage Control store on East Main Street. The woman behind the counter was talking to a smiling, leathery bantam of a man in jeans and a long-sleeved cotton shirt with the sleeves rolled up.

She turned to me when I walked up to the counter, and I asked how business was doing. She nodded at the man and said, "He's got the best corn in town. When he brings it in, I put up a sign that says 'Griff's Corn' and it just flies out of here. Some people buy five dozen ears and put some of it up."

Griff appeared to be a cheerful sort, and after a brief introduction I told him I was working on a story about Andrews and asked if he'd be willing to do an interview.

"Sure," he said.

It was another stellar morning, but not too hot to sit in the car with the windows down and talk. He told me his name was Lawrence Griffing and he was 76 years old.

When I asked if he was from Andrews, he said, "No, I'm not originally from here. I'm from Ohio. I came here after I got out of the military. I figured you can't help where you're conceived, but if I lived in Ohio very long I was crazy."

"But why Andrews?"

"Well," he said, "I went to Florida first, but I didn't like it. I like Andrews. A lot of people don't fit here, but I'm a hick. These are country folk. We're raised the same way. After Florida, I felt like this was home. These are my kind of people. I live like these people. Never had any trouble at all. It's quiet. You'll like it. A lot of nice people here."

In 1965, Griff and his wife, Ruth, opened the Lake's End Grill on Lake Nantahala. "Had a big dock, cabins, boats, all that," he said. "We got famous for our Griffburgers. Took five napkins to eat one."

He chuckled.

After selling the restaurant, Griff sold real estate and spent his spare time in his five-acre garden. "Real estate, that was just something to do," he said, "but I love gardening."

He grimaced. "I plowed my first corn under. Wasn't a good stand. Probably shouldn't have done that, but it just didn't look right. We should have been eating corn by the Fourth of July, and we weren't. But this is the worst year I've ever seen. Germination's been bad, but stuff's coming up now: beets, carrots, peas. I picked seven bushels of beans already. The beans are half-runners, but I don't eat 'em."

"Why not?"

He grimaced again. "I don't like beans with strings in 'em. Like eatin' a hair pie."

That brought livestock to mind. Griff said he had a few head of cattle too.

"I used to do my own butchering, but not anymore," he said. "Now, I have one guy kill it and another guy cut it up. I like the way the second guy cuts the meat. The first guy, you fatten your cow and take it up there, and when you go back to get the meat, there's your old cow smiling at you from a field, and the meat you get is from another, stringy old cow."

We had gotten a little off-topic as far as Andrews was concerned, or so it seemed at first. But then I realized Griff was sharing his life with me. This was what Andrews was about, a man whose passion was working a five-acre garden and grew wonderful Silver Queen corn.

As the interview was ending, Griff insisted that I follow him out to his farm. "Stop by and pick some corn," he said. "Got time now? We'll go up there and I'll get you some stuff. You can't go home empty-handed."

I told Griff that I didn't have time, which wasn't true. I did have time, but his kindness and generosity took me by surprise. I wasn't used to that kind of impulsive behavior, and I had to let it sink in and get comfortable with it.

But two days later I called his home and got Griff's voice on the answer machine: "This is the Griffing residence. Ruth's out moving rocks, and Griff's outstanding in his field."

That was Griff being droll. He clearly said he was "outstanding" in his field, not "out standing" in his field, although at one time or another both were probably true.

He called back later and gave me directions, which I managed not to follow. After driving nearly the entire length of Pisgah Road—a long loop—I had to flag down a van and ask the driver for directions to Phillips Creek Road.

"Follow me," she said.

She turned around, and I followed her a few miles to a rise where the road widened out. She circled, stopped, and pointed. There, 20 yards from Beardog Road, was Phillips Creek Road and Griff's home.

I thanked her, and she waved and drove back in the direction we had just come from. I wondered how far out of her way she had gone to lead me to Griff's place when she could have given me directions and gone on about her business.

Griff was right. There were a lot of nice people in Andrews.

I turned into the long driveway of a pleasant two-story stone and frame house on 21 acres almost in the shadow of the mountains. A deck with a roof ran the length of the house and looked out over a placid green pond. Baskets of flowers hung from the eaves.

Ruth, Griff's wife of 55 years, was on the deck snipping dead leaves off potted plants hanging from roof beams. Across the driveway, Griff was on an orange tractor mowing between tall rows of corn and sunflowers while three plump Jack Russell terriers raced up and down the rows, noses to the ground.

When he saw me, he turned off the tractor and climbed down. The dogs settled around him in the grass, tongues out and panting.

"They look pretty well fed," I said.

He nodded.

"They eat corn," he said. "Snoop"—he gestured at Snoopy, the black and white one—"eats it a row at a time, just like we do. He eats a row, then rolls it over with his paw."

Griff said his corn would be ready to eat in another week, despite being planted late. He overwhelmed me with a basket of corn and other vegetables that would last me a month, all the while apologizing for his unconventional approach to gardening.

"Others here—the old people—plant by the moon and the signs," he said. "Certain crops you plant by the light of the moon—they're above-ground crops—and some by the dark of the moon. Those are below-ground. Me, I don't pay any attention to that. I'm more of a hit-and-miss guy. I go by when it's ready, and I get by."

It was another flawless day. The towering mountains behind him were an immense, comforting presence, and the sun poured its abundance on Griff as he stood there, hands on hips, surveying his happiness.

"Everybody says I'm too old, I should quit farming," he said, squinting up at me. "Maybe I'm a jerk, but I'd just as soon die in a field as a bed."

Chapter 13

Forgive and Forget

Heat was still radiating up from the pavement in front of the Bradley Inn when I climbed into Tony Caivano's pickup. It was nearly 7 p.m. in mid-July, and the sun was still high in a cloudless sky, but angling toward the mountains strung out to the west of town.

Scott Freel had invited us to dinner at his house, which, like Griff Griffing's place, was off Pisgah Road. On the way, we passed a man raking his lawn. He paused to wave to us. A few moments later, we passed a woman walking to her house from the mailbox. She, too, nodded and waved.

I wondered at what point neighborliness became an obligation and maybe even tedious in such a small community. But it seemed like something a cynical city-dweller would ask, so I didn't.

"A lot of people with the same name live in the same part of town," Caivano said. "There are a lot of Hardins up Beaver Creek and a lot of Hydes up this way."

I told Caivano that Jo Jones at the Bradley Inn was amazed when I told her that I was having dinner at Freel's house. "She said that she'd lived here for three years, and only been to Freel's house twice," I said.

"I've known Freel for ten years," Caivano said. "I've never been up there."

Freel lived amid a cluster of new, upscale homes on the lower flank of a long, wooded ridge. It was the only gated development I'd seen in Andrews, although each time I had driven past the gate was open.

The house was a handsome two-story structure, gray with white trim and tucked into a hillside. There was a swimming pool off to the side and, below it a scaled-down barn with the same color scheme as the house. Next to the barn was a corral, a nod to one of Freel's hobbies: riding and working cutting horses.

Freel met us at the front door and led us through a thickly carpeted living room to a bright, airy kitchen. On the counter were a head of lettuce and other vegetables where he had been making a salad. Three potatoes wrapped in aluminum foil lay on the counter next to three filets on a platter.

He had told us at coffee that morning that his wife was out of town, so it would be just the three of us.

As he opened a package of rolls, a phone rang in the next room. When he came back, he said, "I've got to go into town after dinner. Guy needs a water tank."

We ate on an enclosed, air-conditioned porch between the kitchen and a deck. When we finished, Freel suggested that we wait by the pool while he went down to his store. Instead, we told him we'd go along with him and climbed into his pickup.

It was raining when we pulled into the parking lot at Freel Builders Supply. A guy in khaki shorts, a black T-shirt, and hiking boots was waiting under the roof's overhang. I pegged him to be in his late 20s. Tom (not his real name) was tall and sturdy and had dark, placid eyes.

"Hey, Scott," he said, shaking Freel's hand. "Thanks for comin' down."

He shook hands with Caivano, whom he knew from high school, and with me when we were introduced.

It took just a few minutes to find a tank for Tom's toilet, and we were back outside under the overhang. Tom put the tank in his pickup and joined us on the sidewalk. He didn't offer to pay for the tank, and Freel didn't act like he was expecting to be paid.

It reminded me that when I was interviewing Freel in his office a guy had interrupted us to ask how much he owed for some paint. Standard operating procedure seemed to be that customers settled their bill when they had the money, when it was convenient, or both. Not to pay, of course, was unthinkable, but there was no hurry.

Tom and Caivano then began what I had noticed was a powerful custom in Andrews. I came to think of it as "visiting."

Caivano: "You remember Johnny Walker's boy, Walter? You know, the one who married that girl from Marble who got hit by a car?"

Tom: "Sure. Her sister moved to Hayesville with that mechanic?"

Caivano: "Yeah, well, now he's married to that girl who was married to Ronnie Williams—the one with the wall-eye—but they divorced? She used to look really good, but she's gone downhill fast. Drugs and smoking, I heard. And her sister, Esther Lee, is living with Shooter Collins. You know him? His mother went to school with that ol' boy who drives a truck for the county. . . ."

The names and events are fictitious, but the conversation was real.

Visiting—at the post office, in a restaurant, at church, on the road with cars headed in opposite directions, at Freel Builders Supply on a rainy Thursday night—was the fabric of social intercourse in Andrews. It kept communications alive, sustained the town's oral history, and strengthened the sense of community.

But there was a fascinating twist in this case, and it made Freel's willingness to help Tom even more remarkable.

Driving back up to his house, Freel told us that Tom used to work for him.

"He started work on a Wednesday," Freel said, "and we told him he had to work Thursday, Friday, and Saturday. Well, Thursday he came to work and said, 'Now, Scott, do you need me on Saturday?' and I said, 'Yeah, Tom, you gotta work Saturday.' Friday he came to work and at the end of the day, he said, 'Now when do you need me again?' and I said, 'Tom, you gotta work tomorrow. I need you. Margaret is sick and I've got two people out.'

"Well, Saturday comes around and Tom doesn't show up. No sign of him. No calls, nothin'. But Monday, he comes in like nothin' happened. I called him into my office and I said, 'Tom, I don't know how in the world I'm gonna get along without you, but startin' this mornin' I'm gonna find out.'"

That episode, more than anything else I had encountered, demonstrated what made Andrews different. If something like that happened in Atlanta . . . well, it wouldn't. Atlanta is too big, too impersonal. People in Atlanta don't have time for it.

In Atlanta, Tom gets fired and disappears, and in a city that big maybe he and his former employer never see each other again. And if they should ever think of each other after that, most likely it would be with some level of irritation if not downright animosity. Loose ends like that add up and contribute to the stress and friction that fray urban life.

Freel's willingness to go out of his way to help Tom and then to hang out with him afterward struck me as a small miracle. I couldn't tell if he had forgiven Tom or was bemused that Tom would call him when he was in need just a few years after he had let Freel down in his time of need.

But Freel was operating within the customs and wisdom of his culture, and he responded generously. In Andrews, the understanding seemed to be that it's better to forgive and forget. And if you haven't really forgiven and forgotten, pretend. In time, there may be no difference.

Chapter 14

Mountain Spring

I returned to Andrews again a month later and found that August in Andrews was pretty much like August in Atlanta: hot, hazy, and utterly lacking in subtlety. The mountains were almost obscured by haze, and puddles stood in the parking lot at Freel Builders Supply where vehicles had dripped moisture from air conditioners.

This was my third visit to Andrews, and Freel's place was my first stop. I found him in the stockroom sitting on an overturned plastic pail and talking to two bearded men in work clothes. He told them he had seen hunters using dogs to drive deer toward another hunter who was waiting in a pickup.

The disgust in his voice was unmistakable. "Tell you what, though," he said. "You hear dogs drivin' deer, you better be ready. And they don't have to be close. But if it comes my way, I'm gonna shoot that deer, I don't care who's in that truck."

We went back to his office and found a tall, dark-haired man in a sport coat and tie waiting. Freel introduced me to Gene Farley, a friend of Freel's since high school. It was the first time that I'd seen anyone in Andrews wearing a coat and tie.

Farley, it turned out, had an insurance business in Murphy. They chatted briefly about a business matter, and then Freel looked at me.

"He had colon cancer," he said, nodding at Farley. "He isn't supposed to be here."

Farley smiled and nodded, but said nothing. It was quiet for a moment, and Freel got a pained look on his face. "They made an announcement in church Sunday," he said. "One of the people in the congregation has cancer. It's a high school girl."

He paused again. "It's inoperable."

Freel choked up, lowered his head, and stared at his desk. Farley shook his head.

We sat there in silence. Cancer was the elephant in the room.

My father died of a form of cancer called mesothelioma when he was 59. My mother died of breast cancer at 64. I was 55. Even without knowing that in the coming years one of my daughters and one of my brothers would get cancer, I wondered if, as the oldest of five siblings, I was next.

Freel's father was deceased too; was it cancer? I didn't know, but it was possible. And here was Farley, one of his best friends, barely into his forties by the looks of him. And Farley's encounter with cancer was so recent and so vivid that he didn't want to talk about it.

Finally, Farley got up and said, "I've got to get back to the office."

It was well past 11 a.m.—Freel's lunch time—so he and I drove to Chestnuts Café where Caivano joined us.

It was the third time I'd had lunch with Freel and Caivano, and it seemed so natural one might have thought we'd been doing it for years. I didn't give it much thought at the time, nor did it occur to me that at some point during my visits my status in Andrews had changed.

I was no longer a newcomer, no longer a novelty, no longer someone they were wary of. My ever-present pen and notebook notwithstanding, I was someone they liked and trusted enough to spend time with. In fact, Freel's comments about the girl with cancer and his show of emotion was itself a sign of trust. I hadn't seen many men do that ever, whether in Andrews, Atlanta, or anywhere else.

And the feelings were mutual. During all those gatherings over coffee I had heard their banter, their concerns, and their opinions. I had been to their offices. I knew their stories, more or less. I had even been to Freel's home. I admired both of them for what they had accomplished, and I liked them.

But there was nothing in my notes about being accepted, or how I felt about them. It's not that I was unaware of it. I was very much aware of their approval and I was grateful, but I still didn't understand or see the significance of it. My focus was still on Andrews and the people I met. I still thought it was their story I was working on, not mine.

After ordering from the laminated menus, Caivano looked through the window and saw a man in the parking lot. "That guy is two steps short of a staircase," he said.

Freel nodded, saying that the man had once accused the woman who paid his bills and handled his affairs of cheating him. It was an accusation, Freel said, that everyone knew was absurd.

"He made her cry," Freel said. "When I heard that, I found him and grabbed him and pushed him up against the wall and said, 'Your mama don't like you. Your sister don't like you. The only people who like you are your grandmother and [the woman who helps him], and you've made her mad. If I hear you doing that again, I'm gonna come over here and stomp the shit out of you.'

"He said, 'Oh, I won't, Scott. I won't.'"

After lunch, Freel said to me, "Let's go for a ride."

We drove out Fairview Road past the vacant Baker Furniture plant. There was one car in the parking lot, an old beat-up sedan. I asked Freel about it.

"Belongs to the security guard," Freel said.

I said, "I've moved several times, and I've always run into the NFH syndrome—Not From Here. Is that a problem around here?"

"It is and it isn't," he said, stroking his goatee. "I've got neighbors, and he's from Chicago and she's from Florida, and they couldn't be nicer people. They're happy to be here, and they want to fit in.

"On the other hand, there are people like a friend at the hardware store told me about. He said a guy was walkin' around the store sayin', 'There are a lot of assholes in this town.' And my friend said, 'Yeah, but after the first frost, they all go back to Florida.'"

We pulled up in front of a farmhouse with a barn and a garage in back. Freel said it was the home of his friend, Lawrence Hyde. He went to the front door and knocked. A grandmotherly woman wearing an apron answered and held the storm door ajar while they talked.

Freel got back in the truck and turned onto a dirt driveway that led past the house and an oversized garage to a small pasture with a wooden gate. He got out, opened the gate, got back in, drove through, got out again, and closed the gate.

"Three guys riding in a pickup," he said as he slid behind the wheel, "which one's the cowboy?"

"I'm guessing the guy in the middle, but I don't know why."

"Don't have to drive, don't have to open the gates."

We drove through a pasture edged by stands of trees to another gate.

"Want me to get it?" I said.

"Naw," he said. "I'll get it."

At a third gate, Freel parked and we walked through a smaller gate to a shady grove where a small mobile home and three other small buildings formed an intimate camp. Although the temperature was in the 90s, it was cool in the grove, almost damp.

"This is a camp Lawrence and I built," Freel said. "Sometimes we'll come up here for a night or a couple of nights just to relax."

"But this can't be much more than 15 minutes from your house," I said, "and that's if there's a cow in the road on the way."

"Yeah," he said, "but it's not home. Nobody bothers us here."

Beneath a small tree was a pond with several fish eight to ten inches long.

"Trout," Freel said.

He pulled out a bag of pellets and dropped some in the water. The fish ignored them.

He crossed the clearing to a gabled building about the size of a utility shed. Inside were two single beds, one against each wall and separated by a narrow aisle. Against the back wall was a small nightstand.

"This is Margaret's and my place," he said.

He got two folding lawn chairs from a closet, locked the door, and carried them out to the pickup.

Coming back through the gate, he said, "Come over here," jerking his head. "Want to show you something."

I followed him behind the mobile home to what looked like the back of a large, rectangular sign lying on the ground. But there were hinges on it, and a handle.

He grabbed the handle and swung the board away. Beneath it was a hole neatly encased in a squared-off top of spotless gray concrete blocks that looked as if they were new. The hole itself was filled with water so clear and motionless that I thought at first it was covered with glass.

On a ledge a few inches above the water, head erect, was a brown lizard about five inches long. Its tail and slender body glistened in the dappled light, and its abdomen expanded and contracted rapidly. Otherwise it was motionless.

Freel turned to a bush and pulled a mason jar off the end of a branch. He dipped it in the water, filling it halfway.

"This is a mountain spring," he said. "Know how to tell if it's okay to drink?"

I shook my head.

He nodded at the lizard, still motionless on the ledge. "The lizard," he said. "If there's a spring lizard, it's okay."

He drank the water, refilled the jar halfway, and handed it to me. The water was cool, clean, and refreshing. I drank all of it.

Chapter 15

White Wedding

The next day I drove up Junaluska Road to see the shotgun-toting hermit, Bob McClure. He was out in his garden knocking down weeds with a weed whacker and didn't see me arrive. When I whistled he looked up, smiled, and turned off the machine.

As we shook hands, he peered at me with an expression so open and childlike that he almost looked as if he were mentally disabled. Remembering the knowing looks I'd gotten in town when I mentioned his name, I said, "Do you remember me?"

"Sure do," he said with a slow smile. "John Christensen. C'mon in."

The front door opened into a small, dark living room with two overstuffed love seats against adjoining walls. Between them, partially blocking the doorway to the kitchen and another to a bedroom, was a worn and faded recliner.

There were shoes and a baseball cap on the linoleum floor, which was old and worn and looked like it needed sweeping. The air was heavy with decades of cooking odors. Against the right-hand wall were two televisions, an old-fashioned, console-style floor model and a smaller table model on the floor in front of it.

The front half of the room was dominated by a wide, waist-high furnace on top of which were trays with bottles of Tums, Rolaids, and various medications. A galvanized pipe rose from the rear of the furnace and disappeared into the ceiling.

Hanging over the front window was an American flag upon which had been superimposed the image of a Native American warrior on horseback and brandishing a rifle. The image reminded me that, on our first meeting, McClure had referred to "the Great Spirit." Given his dark hair and eyes and tawny skin, I wondered if he might be Native American.

Beyond the living room, sunlight pouring through two windows lit up a small kitchen. On the wall above the sink were three ceramic plates, one of them bearing a likeness of Jesus of Nazareth.

I told McClure that on this visit my focus was Andrews rather than the manhunt, and wanted to know more about his background. He said that his grandfather had built the house and that he had inherited it from his mother when he returned from years of wandering that took him as far as Wilmington on the North Carolina coast.

"I worked in sawmills and made $500 a day cutting locust wood," he said. "That's mighty tough wood to cut."

He also worked in a textile mill dyeing cloth before returning to Andrews to work in the plant that made Lee clothing. Ruptured discs in his back forced him out of work and disabled him.

"I'm also deaf in one ear," he added, "and I don't hear too good out of the other one."

I wondered if people misunderstood McClure, if perhaps his hearing problems might account for his childlike manner. Few things are more isolating than the inability to understand what people are saying. What seemed like eccentricity might simply be his attempts to lip-read what he couldn't hear. Eventually it's easier not to ask people to repeat themselves, and easier still to keep to yourself, which is what McClure had done.

"Did you have any experience with Rudolph or the law enforcement people?" I asked.

"Two FBI agents came here and wanted to know if I'd seen Rudolph," he said. "I told them if I ever saw him, I wouldn't know him. And that I didn't care if he blows all the abortion clinics up, but don't hurt no people."

He pulled a worn wallet from his back pocket, fished out a card, and handed it to me. Embossed on it was the FBI shield with the name Special Agent Ronald G. Pool. Penned below it was "Kirk Henry."

"They were real nice," he said. "They didn't search or nothin'. One of them asked me if I go to church. I said, 'Three hundred and sixty-five days a year. The body is the temple of the Holy Spirit.'"

In a singsong voice, he switched to Scripture: "Nicodemus said to Jesus, 'I am too old, how can I be reborn?' Jesus said, 'The wind comes. You can hear it, but you cannot see it.'"

He smiled. "My duty and yours is to become as much God-like as we can. That's in Genesis. I think you're supposed to search deep within yourself. It's between you and your Maker."

McClure went into the bedroom and returned with a photo album. He flipped it open to a picture of himself from 20 years earlier and handed it to me. He had dark, wavy hair and a thick beard in those days, and looked remarkably like a rough-hewn James Garner.

When we first met, McClure had told me about being awake for four days and having an out-of-body experience.

"Do you remember anything more about that?" I asked.

"I was drinking," he said. "I didn't tell you that before." He paused and shook his head. "It was a bad time—the long, dark night of the soul."

But afterward, he said, he went nine and a half years "without a drop. Wife left me. Met another woman and we had a daughter. That's Jessica's mother."

Jessica, he said, was now 12.

"But you drink now?" I said. "You were drinking a beer last time I was here."

He nodded. "I was told I was a chronic alcoholic, but I must be cured, because that's all I want."

He smiled. He was still thinking about that out-of-body experience. "That was peace," he said. "And the bluest sky you ever saw, and that great white light. . . ."

He was quiet for a time, the silence of a man accustomed to his own company.

"Do you have any other kids?"

"Beside Jessica, I've got a son and two other daughters," he said. "They're all adults. They come see me sometimes, but mostly I'm alone."

Another pause.

"I'm a loner," he said. "I don't have nothing to do with the neighbors. I hunt alone and people say, 'Aren't you afraid?' But I'm never afraid. I'm never by myself. They're always with me."

I assumed he meant angels, so I didn't say anything.

"People think I'm a nut," he said, "but after that experience. . . ."

He thought for a moment. "It's like what this guy said about me. He said, 'He gets to fly free.'" He smiled. "Every day I think about that experience. Every day."

Back in Andrews, I drove to Hall Memorial Park, which is just a block off Main Street, and parked. I would be leaving shortly for Atlanta, but I had one more stop to make.

The park was bordered on three sides by streets and by railroad tracks on the fourth. Beyond the tracks were a wide, green field, a faded barn, and then more lush pasture rising toward the mountains.

It amazed me to find such a view one block off the main street, and I wanted to photograph it before I left.

It was mid-afternoon on a Friday, and as I walked into the park, a man was setting up rows of folding metal chairs near a gazebo. "My daughter's getting married," he said to a passing woman.

By the time I crossed to the other side of the park, snapped a few photographs, and returned, several women in dresses had seated themselves in the first two rows of chairs. A few rows behind them were two men wearing short-sleeved shirts and ties. In the row behind them were two small boys in slacks and T-shirts, and a little girl in a fluffy white dress.

A long table had been set up well back from the chairs, and on it were several covered dishes, paper plates, plastic cups, forks, and two large green bottles of Sprite.

In the gazebo, a heavyset man in suspenders, blue tie, and short-sleeved white shirt stood waiting. He was holding what looked like a Bible or prayer book.

I looked around, wondering where the rest of the guests and the wedding party might be. Although there were twenty-five or thirty chairs, fewer than a dozen were occupied, and the street was empty.

Glancing up and down the street, something white caught my attention. It was the bride in a wedding dress and an older man in a dark suit, presumably her father, waiting in the lobby of the post office for the ceremony to begin.

It was a compelling, small-town scenario about to play itself out, and I wanted to get photos of that as well. I waited at the edge of the park and watched a few more guests arrive, but the wait seemed interminable.

It was well past the top of the hour, and after about 20 minutes, I gave up. I crossed the street, got in my car and eased out of the parking space. As I drove slowly up the street, I glanced at the rearview mirror and there, framed in the reflection, was the National Geographic moment my impatience caused me to miss.

The bride was crossing the street arm in arm with her father. Behind them, the little girl in the fluffy dress was carrying the end of the bride's dress, the long bridal train virginal white against the asphalt background and shimmering with hope.

Chapter 16

Scandal

In November 2000, the FBI engaged in what was becoming an autumn ritual: a press conference asking hunters to watch for signs of Eric Rudolph. It rained heavily that morning, and the press conference was moved from Andrews to the National Guard Armory in Murphy.

It had been two years since anyone had seen Rudolph, and no one from Andrews attended the press conference. I did attend, but only as a formality. Something far more compelling had everyone's attention and brought me back to Andrews.

In October, the Andrews Town Council had fired Jim Dailey from his $28,000-a-year job as town administrator and finance officer. He was also forced to resign his position as mayor, which paid $4,800 a year, and was being investigated by the North Carolina State Bureau of Investigation.

The reason: "misappropriation of funds." Among the charges were that the white, vinyl-covered railing for the front porch of Dailey's new house had been paid for with town funds. So had the newly paved driveway and a propane heater at the home of Bill Stiles, a former town employee and Dailey's friend. Stiles was also Dailey's co-defendant.

Public money had also been spent on tin roofing, roofing nails, vinyl siding, a John Deere mower, and a weed whacker. A check had been forged, invoices were falsified, and the serial numbers on the mower had been filed off.

Now things began to make sense: in particular, the scowling man at my first interview with Dailey, and Dailey's agitation when I interviewed him the second time.

It was a dreary, chilly day, and when I drove into Andrews after the press conference, all the empty storefronts looked as forlorn as the first time I saw them. It was a mood befitting the occasion.

I drove to Freel Builders Supply and found Freel in his office.

"I heard about Jim Dailey," I said.

He shook his head.

"He came to see me the day after he was fired," he said. "He admitted what he had done and he apologized for it. I told him I would not be the one to judge him. That's not for me to do."

He frowned and leaned forward, his chin stopping a few inches from the desktop. It was the third time I'd seen him do that, a mannerism that seemed to allow him time to sort out his thoughts and choose his words.

"But I just don't understand what happened!" he said. "I wonder why he did it if he knew it was wrong?"

"What's Dailey doing now?"

"He's been working for a contractor," he said. "Last I heard, he was pouring concrete, which is a tough, dirty job."

I called Dailey's home, dreading the conversation. The last thing I wanted to do was to make an uncomfortable situation worse, but I had committed to doing a story about Andrews and its people. This was the biggest news in Andrews in a long time. There was no way I could not talk to Jim Dailey.

Dailey's number had been changed and was unlisted. But it was midday and raining, and thinking that he probably wasn't working, I drove to his house.

The white two-story home—the one Dailey told me earlier he'd been reluctant to move into—was located in a flat, treeless field about 100 yards behind a strip of offices on Main Street. A narrow lane ran between the office buildings, passed Dailey's house, and ended 100 yards beyond at a small apartment building.

There was a shiny black pickup in the driveway, and one of the garage doors was open. An aging yellow Labrador retriever came out of the garage, head low and sniffing as I got out of my car, and a moment later Dailey himself emerged.

He smiled and we shook hands, but his face was seamed with fatigue and worry, and his eyes were haunted.

"I heard about what happened," I said.

He nodded. "I hate that this happened," he said. "The town didn't need something like this. I went to the merchants and told them what I did was wrong, and that I was sorry. I told them I wanted them to hear it from me and not from somebody else or the newspaper. I also went to my church and asked them to forgive me. And I asked God to forgive me."

"It takes a lot of courage to do that," I said.

He leaned heavily against the door frame. "It's been hard," he said. "Real hard. It took me 50 years to make a mistake like this, and it's hard to face the people in this town now."

"We all do things we're not proud of," I said. "It's what we do afterward that matters."

He searched my face for a moment, then looked down at his feet.

"There's an investigation going on," he said. "I've been sitting out here trying to remember everything that happened so I can defend myself. I've had to get a lawyer. It's gonna cost me a lot of money."

His eyes were searching, fearful. Then he brightened. "Would you be a character witness for me?"

That was a surprise. I didn't know what to say. I felt sorry for him, no matter what he'd done. I believed he was a good man who had made a mistake. But in my mind I was still a journalist reporting a story, not being part of it.

"That's a tough one, Jim," I said. "If I were subpoenaed, I'd tell the truth. But I don't think I can voluntarily appear as a witness."

The light in his eyes died. I tried to say something reassuring without sounding patronizing, but it didn't help. He had the look of a man on a desert island watching a ship disappear over the horizon.

There wasn't much else to say, and a few minutes later I left. As I pulled away, I glanced back. Dailey was sitting in a lawn chair in the doorway of the garage with a pad and pen in his hand, the picture of dejection.

A month later, Dailey paid the town $3,600 for the roofing materials and porch railing. "I made a mistake," he told the Andrews Journal, "and I'm paying for it. I'm as sorry as I can be, and I'm doing all I can to make it right."

I called the North Carolina Bureau of Investigation's western district in Asheville and spoke to David Barnes, the special agent in charge of the office. I told Barnes that I had spoken with Dailey and he seemed not only ashamed, but also remorseful at the inconvenience he was causing others.

Barnes wasn't impressed.

"Our feeling is that when a person takes an oath when they are elected or appointed to a government position, they are taking on responsibility to the public," Barnes said. "They also agree that they should shoulder a higher level of responsibility because of that trust.

"The value of prosecuting someone who has violated that trust is self-evident: the public loses trust in public institutions every time this happens. I strongly believe, and my agency believes, that people should be made to be accountable for whatever actions they take."

I asked Barnes if Dailey's admission of guilt and the restitution he had made would have any impact on the investigation. "That makes no difference," he said. "Restitution has no effect."

I told Barnes that Dailey said he felt especially sorry for bringing unflattering attention to Andrews.

"Too bad," Barnes said. "We really, in this part of the state—"

He paused for a moment, and started again. "We get stereotyped something awful up here, and it's not fair," he said. "I'm pretty certain he feels bad about it. He's not shining you on about that. This is bringing unneeded publicity to Andrews."

Chapter 17

Fresh Air

On Wednesday, January 24, 2001, two months after my most recent visit to Andrews, I stepped out onto the front porch of my home to let the cat out. It was cold and overcast, the trees were bare, and the ground was littered with brown leaves.

But the smell of fresh air was invigorating and reminded me that I'd been spending too much time indoors. "Man," I said out loud, "I've got to get outside more."

Other than my visits to Andrews, I spent almost my entire workweek inside. CNN Center had two towers and an atrium with a coffee bar, restaurants—mostly fast-food—and a cafeteria. Unless I was meeting someone for lunch, I generally stayed in the building all day every day.

But shortly after I got to the office that morning, my phone rang. It was one of the assistant editors.

"Would you come up to 10 North?" he said.

Uh-oh.

After months of rumors, AOL and TimeWarner, CNN's parent company, had finally merged at the beginning of the year. What was being called "the deal of the century" was also attended by widespread speculation that there were would be layoffs at CNN, and the rumors were true.

On the previous Friday, our editor-in-chief, Scott Woelfel, was the first at CNN Interactive (CNN.com's formal name) to get a pink slip. On Monday, his two immediate subordinates were also tossed over the side.

The result on 10 South, where I worked in special projects, was a scarcely controlled panic and the strangest period of my career. Thirty or 40 people went into a frenzy of activity, and I would have bet the mortgage that none of it was company business.

They were writing résumés, making calls, and shopping online for jobs, because the message was clear: if Woelfel and the others weren't safe, no one was.

The most compelling scenario was watching a woman in her early thirties going from one glass-windowed office to the next with a haggard expression on her face. She had recently had a baby and just returned to work. The offices she visited were occupied by editors. She was begging for her job.

I had done my best not to get caught up in the panic. I did not dash off a résumé, nor did I scramble for another job. I knew I might be laid off, but I had done good work. I had good reviews. I hadn't made any enemies, and I had even coached some of the younger writers.

It wasn't that I was overly confident. But over the past year I had been visited repeatedly by the thought that it was time to leave, that there was something else I must do, and it wasn't about getting another job.

I might have regarded this notion as merely a rogue thought were it not for a couple of unusual experiences. One occurred as I made my way to work one morning in the glacial experience known as Atlanta traffic.

Infuriated at the crawl and without thinking I shouted, "This is not what my life is about!"

The other occurred on a Saturday afternoon on the way to visit a friend. I stopped at a coffee shop in Midtown, and as I walked across the parking lot, it hit me. This was how I wanted to live and work—keeping my own schedule, not punching a clock, going for coffee when I wanted, any time of day, any day of the week.

Going to Andrews had been my only assignment out of the building in five years. Everything else I'd done—research, interviews, writing—was done by computer or phone at a desk. True, I was making more money than ever, but I was getting restless.

So I wasn't clinging to my job as I headed for the elevator to 10 North. I was two months away from my 56th birthday and still drifting.

By the time I crossed the mezzanine from the south tower to the north, I had no doubt what was about to happen. It was confirmed when I got to the elevator, and there waiting for it was my editor, Wright Bryan.

"Oh, no," I said, "Do you think they'll give us time for a cigarette before they shoot us?"

On 10 North, I found a young guy I'd never seen before sitting at a desk. He couldn't have been more than 25, and his suit was so new it was radioactive. He introduced himself and said he was from Human Resources.

Next to him and seated behind the same desk was an older guy, the editor who had called me. The two of them sitting behind the same desk looked ridiculous, and I was tempted to go for sarcasm (from the Greek word sarkasmos [tearing flesh]) and applaud them for saving the company money by sharing a desk.

Instead, I ruminated on the fact that before the editor was hired he had come for an interview, and I had shown him around the building. Now here he was showing me the door.

The kid delivered the news: I was no longer employed, effective immediately. I would turn in my building pass down the hall, get a temporary pass, and had until the end of the day to collect my belongings and leave.

The editor leaned forward and said with a straight face, "We looked everywhere, but we couldn't find anything for you."

This, of course, was bullshit, a great steaming pile thereof. The exercise was cutting costs. I was one of the highest-paid writers on the staff. If he'd had the stones to say, "We can't afford you, you're too expensive," I'd have shaken his hand and offered to buy him a beer after work.

Instead, given the dissembling and commitment to mediocrity, all I could muster was contempt.

The kid went on. I would be getting five months' severance and short-term health insurance . . . and my thoughts drifted away.

I glanced up at the ceiling. It was about 20 feet high and sloped upward from left to right as the tower narrowed toward the top. The ceiling itself and the pipes running just below it had been sprayed with an industrial coating the color of river mud. Fire retardant, I thought.

Then another, more provocative realization: I was going to have forty hours a week to kill. What was I going to do with all that time?

When the charade was over, I walked down the hallway to a room where a woman took my building pass and gave me a temporary pass. She reminded me that the pass would expire that night.

Heading back to the elevators, I passed a room where two burly black men in sport coats and ties were watching TV. They looked familiar. Then I recognized them. They were security guards. We often worked out at the same time at the health club in the basement, but I'd only seen them in exercise clothing or uniforms.

Then I realized they were on hand in case someone had a violent reaction to losing their job. The coats and ties were a clever touch, a passive request for decorum and civility.

When I walked in, they looked up and smiled. Then one of them saw the temporary pass hanging from my belt. "Oh, no," he said, "they got you?"

"Yeah, they did."

"Oh, no . . ."

"Yeah . . . well . . . it's all part of growing up, right?"

There wasn't much to say. They wished me well, and I wished them well. We shook hands and said goodbye.

Back on 10 South, I found a box and cleaned out my desk. I was out of the building in less than two hours, and I was in the parking garage when reality landed. I had bought a three-year-old Audi A4 six months earlier. I loved the car. Now I was going to have to find a way to pay for it.

There was a party that evening at a bar in the Virginia-Highlands neighborhood. On my way to the party, I got a preview of the emotions to come in the next several months.

I was listening to music, and suddenly it hit me: Wow! I don't have to go to work tomorrow!

I threw my hands up and cheered.

Minutes later, I was thinking how this was the first time in my life I had lost my job. Technically I had been laid off, but it felt like I'd been fired and it infuriated me. I hadn't done anything wrong. In fact, I was damn good, and being treated this way was unjust and unfair.

Rejection was a deep, old wound, and burning still—I wasn't good enough, wasn't smart enough, wasn't lovable enough—and I erupted in a roaring, cursing rage. Unfortunately, there was no one on hand to point out that I had raged a year ago about having to commute, and now I was raging about losing that commute.

Irony aside, outbursts like that repeated themselves over and over in the coming months. I'd be up one moment, down the next. Okay for a few hours; depressed for many more.

The party that night was initially called to say goodbye to Woelfel, but in four days so many people had been laid off it took on the air of a mass wake. When I saw Bruce Kennedy, one of my favorite coworkers, he said, "Damn! They got you, too? All the good people are leaving."

"Bruce," I said, "you've got a wife and kid. You need the job."

Wandering around the dimly lit room, I kept running into people I knew and liked. As an athlete growing up, being part of a team was my favorite of all things. It was my tribe, the one place where it felt safe to be myself. I wasn't that close with the people at the party. The bond wasn't as intense, but we had worked together with a singular purpose. Seeing them in this different and oddly charged setting, I was already beginning to grieve losing those connections.

A few months later, I went for a walk one evening and ran into Fred Tasse. Fred worked in information technology at CNN, but I knew him better from the neighborhood. His evening routine involved walking a big, shaggy mutt named Rocco. This time Fred's wife was with them, too.

"Hey," he said, "I haven't seen you around lately. . . ." His voice tailed off. "Wait, did you get laid off?"

"Yeah," I said, and gave them a brief summary.

His wife said, "Are you going to take a vacation?"

"God, no!" I said. "I've got to find a job!"

Good luck with that. It was March 2001. The dot-com bubble that resulted from massive speculation in online companies was beginning to deflate. The stock market was in the early stages of a 78 percent nosedive, sending dozens of companies to their graves. Many of them were communications companies, and the media that survived went on an industry-wide bender to cut costs. Lucky employees got buyouts or severance; the unlucky got only a pink slip.

I was lucky. I got severance, temporary health insurance, and a nonnegotiable reminder that it was time to move on. And it didn't hurt my feelings when the AOL/TimeWarner merger that was initially hailed as "the deal of the century" two years later was relabeled "the worst deal of the century."

Chapter 18

Hope

The next several months were ugly. I fretted and churned about money, an issue that was always bubbling in the background when I had income and boiled to the surface when money was scarce.

To rid myself of car payments, I paid off the loan. That put a deep dent in my savings, which had been growing slowly after a divorce, two moves, and a stretch where I was between jobs. Unfortunately, it didn't have the desired effect.

Rather than being relieved at eliminating a significant monthly expense, my overactive imagination went looking for trouble elsewhere. It found it in the other big-ticket item in my budget: the mortgage.

In 1997 I had bought a 1924 bungalow in an old neighborhood that was showing signs of gentrification. The neighborhood was gentrifying, that is, not the house. The house needed work, but I was grateful to have it. I had moved seven times since college and twice after getting to Atlanta. I'd lived in apartments and a duplex, and shared a small house with a girlfriend.

Buying a house was one of the few times where it felt like I was doing something sensible, the behavior of a normal person with a regular life. In a neighborhood where tearing houses down was going viral, I had looked forward to fixing mine up. When the layoff occurred I had been nearing the point financially where I could start making some of those repairs.

There was a 15-year ARM on the house, and when it expired, the interest rate would go up significantly. There were still eleven years to go, which is plenty of time to the rational mind, but my thoughts were not entirely my own. At no time in my life did I consider myself normal or my life regular.

Twenty-six hundred years ago, the Greek playwright Euripides wrote, "The gods visit the sins of the fathers upon the children." I would amend it to say the pain of the parents is visited upon the children.

My father grew up in a family that was, as my cousin put it, "dirt poor." His mother immigrated from Northern Ireland in 1909 and worked as a maid. His father was a factory worker and later a farmer and carpenter.

My grandfather was also, if an experience I had with him was any indication, a stealth drinker.

My father worked in a grocery store after high school and put himself through a technical college at night. He worked hard—although I never saw that it gave him much pleasure—and made a lot of money. He died from cancer two months after his 59th birthday. At the funeral reception, one of his former minions, flush with a buzz from my father's bourbon, said, "Your father had deep pockets and short arms."

My mother's father was an ornery alcoholic who lost his job in the Depression. At eight, my mother was sent two states away to live with an uncle who didn't want her. She never got over the experience. Losing her husband when she was 58 was the final proof that life was unfair.

Every time I hear someone say, "This, too, shall pass," I think of my mom. She used to say it all the time, but to her the light at the end of the tunnel was a train coming the other way. She died at 64, also from cancer.

My mother shared a little of her past. My father shared even less. They never talked about their feelings or failures or the lessons they had learned, something I've noticed in others of their generation. Life was something you survived and tried to forget, not a Disney movie.

As the oldest of five sons I bought into the family angst early on and spent the rest of my life trying to fight my way out. I spent the first months after the layoff tiptoeing through a minefield of emotions. Some fears were genuine, many more were imagined, but always I was in survival mode.

Thus, no car payment? No problem. Given the stock market decline, the dying companies, the shrinking journalism profession, my unemployable age, and the mortgage, an enormous and ominous cloud hovered over me.

It wasn't that I was bereft of resources. I considered writing a book, perhaps riffing off Rick Warren's tome about the purpose-driven life. Something to the effect that, "If you do what you love, the money will come."

I dusted off an idea for a TV documentary series that I had submitted to PBS before CNN.com hired me. I had mentioned the idea to Deepak Chopra while interviewing him for a story. Chopra was interested, and after the layoff I called him back.

Chopra and his daughter had started a TV production company. They were looking for ideas, and I was looking for a place to land, another employer. Working with someone as smart and successful as Chopra seemed like answered prayer.

Still, I was guarded in our telephone conversations, not giving much away. Looking back on it, I can't imagine why he hung in there with me as long as he did. I don't think I said anything of substance, and when I concluded that he wasn't looking for employees, I backed away.

I thought at the time I didn't trust Chopra, but the truth was I didn't trust myself. I lacked the entrepreneurial drive and confidence to participate at his level. I was still looking for easy answers, still drifting, a long way from reconciling with the new reality.

I was also two decades into my quest for belonging, sanity, and serenity. I grew up in Presbyterian and Congregational churches, went to a Baptist college (Wake Forest), and undertook a walkabout as an adult that led into some strange spiritual corners.

In early adulthood, I did my share of partying but never stopped searching for something meaningful and lasting. But as long as I was employed and collecting a regular paycheck, my spiritual pursuits were a hobby. I still hadn't found what I was looking for, as Bono put it in a U2 song, but there wasn't any urgency either.

In Atlanta, I found my way to a Unity church and considered its low-key, mind-over-matter approach reasonable and sensible. But after the layoff I discovered that reasonable and sensible aren't much help when your hair is on fire.

That's where things stood in mid-May 2001 when I awoke in the middle of the night, sat bolt upright, and blurted out, "Jesus, I'm scared!"

Jesus got little if any attention at Unity, but I'd been reading a richly detailed account of his life in a 2,100-page cosmology called the Urantia Book, so I wasn't just grasping for names on the wheel of fortune.

This was one of those "there are no atheists in foxholes" moments. The fear and despair I struggled to bottle up during the day had erupted. I needed help. Stripped of the mask of adulthood, alone in the dark where everything seems huge and hostile, I called out to the kindest, strongest, and most loving person I'd ever heard of.

Ordinarily, an experience like that would keep me awake for hours, looking for hope but obsessed with fearful scenarios and dire consequences.

But something amazing happened. Warmth and peace settled around me like a blanket, wrapping me in blissful languor. I felt safe, whole, complete. It felt like I was in the lap of God, which was so astonishing that—ever the journalist—I wanted to say or do something to acknowledge or document the moment. But I felt so warm and loved that I couldn't keep my eyes open. It was as if I'd been drugged. I laid back down and fell into a deep, beautiful, dreamless sleep.

I wish I could say that experience changed my life, but morning dawned pretty much the way it always did. The mortgage was still there, and I had no plan to pay for it. I didn't have a woman in my life for moral support or a hug. I had nothing to look forward to except more of the same.

And yet while I was not transformed, I can't say that I wasn't changed by that middle-of-the-night rescue. Not everyone gets a burning bush. For some, change takes time and the long way around, building hope one day at a time.

But there are encouraging signs along the way, and I was certain about one thing: I would never forget that experience.

Chapter 19

Judgment

By October 2001 I was thinking about Andrews again. It had been eleven months since my last visit. I was settling into my new life and had sold a few freelance articles. It occurred to me that once completed, the Andrews story might find a home at a national magazine.

I had plenty of material, but I didn't yet have a resolution. Something was missing, something that would tie up the loose ends and pull the story together. One of the things I wanted resolution on was the Jim Dailey situation.

Dailey and his co-defendant, Bill Stiles, had gone to trial just a few weeks earlier. If I had known about the trial, I would have attended it myself.

But even before I returned to the town, I learned that Dailey's trial had played out in a way that was quintessentially Andrews.

The trial was held on September 18 in Murphy. Although Murphy was 14 miles from Andrews, nearly one hundred people had put aside their everyday concerns to make the trip and show up in court on a Tuesday morning.

Malfeasance was not the issue that day. Dailey and Stiles had agreed to plead guilty. The only question was punishment, and anyone attending in the spirit of Old Testament justice was doomed to disappointment.

Dailey's attorney, Reid Brown, put five people on the stand that morning: a Baptist minister, two highway patrolmen, the chief of police, and a county commissioner. Every one of them testified that they had known Jim Dailey for years and that he was a good man.

Perhaps the most compelling witness that afternoon was a building contractor named Dick Strahan. It was Strahan who gave Dailey the job of pouring concrete after the town fired him. Strahan told the court, "I would trust Jim with anything I have."

If Brown had asked random spectators in the courtroom to testify, there is little doubt that they also would have voiced their support for Dailey.

He was born and raised in Andrews. He went to school in Andrews. When he left the army, he made his home in Andrews. He coached the high school basketball team in Andrews. He and his family attended Second Baptist Church in Andrews.

And when Jim Dailey had his day in court, the people of Andrews closed ranks around one of their own.

The unmistakable message was that Jim Dailey was a good man. He was a lifelong member of the community, a friend and neighbor who attended church three times a week in a town where that was the ultimate compliment. But he was also human. He made a mistake, he owned up to it, and he made restitution. Enough said.

Dailey and Stiles were given suspended sentences along with probation, community service, and financial penalties. But the people of Andrews had already rendered their judgment. They had moved on.

Chapter 20

Hard Work

It was a bright and sunny day when I returned to Andrews in early October 2001. It felt good to be back, and I was curious to see if anything had changed.

There were still "For Sale" and "For Rent" signs in the same empty buildings on Main Street, but there was a bright new awning over the door of a computer shop. There were also new awnings above the store windows across the street from the Bradley Inn.

Out on East Main Street, just down the block from Trammel Quick Stop and Feed Supply, a storefront wore a dazzling new coat of white paint and a bold, colorful sign announcing Imaginations Tattoo and Body Piercings.

They were modest improvements, to be sure, but they were improvements nonetheless.

It was also just a month after the September 11 terrorist attacks, and a few days after the United States had begun bombing suspected terrorist bases in Afghanistan. When I got to Freel Builders Supply that morning, Caivano was in Freel's office telling him what he had missed earlier at the coffee shop.

"Ray Rowles said he didn't agree with us bombing Afghanistan," Caivano said with an air of disapproval.

"Really?" Freel drawled. "That surprises me. Back when I was teaching school, I told 'em if they did somethin' wrong I'd bust their ass. So they didn't do it. Same thing."

Caivano said he had tried to reason with Rowles, but to no avail. "I guess he was in Sarasota too long," Caivano said. "Went to his head."

Freel looked at me and said, "What do you think?"

I hesitated. Given their opinions, this wasn't something I wanted to talk about. They had welcomed me back warmly, and in other circumstances I might have begged off just to avoid conflict. But I felt strongly about the issue, and I took a risk.

"I think we ought to do something, but I agree with Ray," I said. "I don't think bombing's the answer. Look what happened in Vietnam. We started bombing over there, got involved in a war we couldn't win and didn't win, and fifty-seven thousand Americans got killed."

Among those killed in Vietnam were my cousin, a college friend, and my friend and quarterback in high school. I didn't tell them that, and I'm not sure why. It might have helped, because the looks on their faces told me I had just dropped a peg in their estimation.

We discussed it for a time, going back and forth without rancor, but also without any signs of change on either side.

After Caivano left, Freel said, "I'm building a house and I've got to go up and measure doorways. Come with me."

With the soundtrack from *O Brother, Where Art Thou?* playing, we drove past the sprawling, empty plant that was last occupied by Baker Furniture. More than a year before, Freel and I had ridden past that plant and the same weather-beaten sedan belonging to the security guard was parked in the same place. And, just as last time, it was the only vehicle in the lot.

What on earth, I wondered, could that guy be doing to keep himself from being bored silly?

Freel drove up Pisgah Road to Fairhaven Drive, a narrow strip of asphalt scarcely wide enough for one vehicle. We climbed a steep ridge past several homes, most of them new. When the asphalt ended, we continued up a rutted gravel road to a spot where a new house wrapped in shiny white insulation gleamed in the morning sun.

While Freel measured doorways, I wandered through the house. It had three floors, a porch in front, a deck in back, and plenty of windows to take in the breathtaking views of the mountains. At this height, the peaks were nearly at eye level.

When he finished, we bounced higher yet to another house. This one was just a foundation, a floor, and two partial walls, but the view was even more spectacular. Across a narrow valley ran an unbroken line of ridges and crests that dropped steeply into forested valleys ablaze with fall color.

Two pickups were parked near the house, one with the driver's door open. Four men stood nearby drinking coffee. One of them was Lawrence Hyde, whose farm included the camp, mountain spring, and spring lizard that Freel had shown me 15 months earlier.

I liked Lawrence. We had met in Freel's office on one of my previous visits, but we hadn't had an opportunity to say much more than hello and goodbye. I wasn't sure that Lawrence cared to talk that much, anyway. He had a quiet dignity and a wry, watchful way that made me think that he was secretly amused by life in general. I understood why Freel valued him as a friend even though Lawrence was at least twenty years older.

"We met last year in Freel's office," I said.

He nodded, and I was flattered to think that he remembered me, or seemed to. He gestured at Freel who was talking to the others. "He tellin' you anything good?"

"Yeah."

His gaze settled on Freel's boots, which were charcoal-gray leather with heavy lug soles. The leather was so clean and unmarked the boots had to be new. "Wears nice boots, don't he?"

"Sure does."

He studied the boots for a moment. "I'll have 'em by evenin'."

I laughed.

He climbed up on a backhoe, turned it on, and went to work on a half-finished trench. After just a few minutes, he switched the machine off again, and climbed down. Picking up a hammer from a toolbox, he knelt in the ditch and began knocking dirt out of a clogged pipe.

Lawrence was still cleaning out the pipe when Freel and I left a few minutes later. I told Freel what Hyde had said about his boots, and he chuckled.

"Tell you what, though," he said. "He's a hard worker. You spend a day workin' with Lawrence, he'll wear your ass out."

That afternoon I drove over to Reid's Place to see Teresa Bateman, and the first thing I noticed was that the restaurant had new pine siding. There was also a second picnic table on the porch, a TV high on the wall tuned to a country music channel, and red, white, and blue bows hanging from the roof beams.

Obviously business was good. But when I went to the window, it wasn't Teresa Bateman who opened it, but her sister, Sheila. Their mother, Wanda Reid, was standing behind her.

"Oh, Teresa's not workin' here anymore," Sheila said. "She sold the restaurant to my brother."

"What's she doing?"

"Singin', mostly. 'Least, that's what she wants to do."

"She was workin' awful hard," Wanda said.

Sheila nodded. "Workin' here about killed her."

She gave me two phone numbers. "I don't know if that first number's still connected," she said, "but the other one's her mother-in-law. They live next door to her."

The first number had indeed been disconnected when I called, but Teresa's mother-in-law answered the second number. She told me to wait while she walked the phone next door. When she gave the phone to Teresa, I could hear a TV in the background.

"So you sold the restaurant," I said.

"I did," she said. "I sold it to my brother, James. I was workin' myself to death. I love my family, but I needed a break."

"What have you been doing since you sold it?"

"Not much," she said. "I've been singin' some, but nothin's changed. But I'm thinkin' about openin' a restaurant in Robbinsville." Her husband, Eldridge, was the sales manager at Jacky Jones Ford in Robbinsville.

"But if you worked so hard here," I said, "wouldn't you do the same thing in Robbinsville?"

"I won't hold the hours I did," she said. "I'll do a lot of things different."

It didn't occur to me until much later, but that conversation was revealing. It was none of my business whether Teresa Bateman opened a restaurant in Robbinsville and worked too hard. But Freel had said that everyone in Andrews was like family, and he was right. I was too close to see it at the time, but I had gotten to know and care about people like Teresa so much that I was acting like a member of the family.

Chapter 21

Piece of Cake

After coffee the next morning, I called Griff Griffing. No drollery this time. Griff himself answered.

"I just baked a cake," he said. "If you come out here, you can have a piece."

I don't usually eat in the morning, but I wanted to talk to Griff so I accepted the invitation. This time I remembered how to get there, and I noticed as I pulled into the driveway that except for a single row of sunflowers, everything in Griff's garden had been plowed under. It being October, that made sense.

This time there were just two Jack Russells, Snoopy and Dixie, on duty and they set up a clamor when I drove up to the house. They were joined by a rangy young German shepherd quivering with nervous energy.

Ruth Griffing came out of the house in jeans and blouse, hair pulled back in a ponytail. She waved to Griff, who was on his tractor pulling a trailer loaded with dead tree limbs.

"I didn't see you drive in," he said. "Come on inside."

Griff and I sat in swivel chairs at the kitchen table while Ruth leaned against the counter in what I imagined was a long-standing farm custom. The men sat and talked. The women stood nearby, taking it all in and contributing where necessary.

It didn't seem to be a sexist distinction as much as deeply held habits based on splitting the labor: the field was Griff's office, the kitchen was Ruth's. But, then, Ruth loved to garden, and what to make of the moist, rich apple cake Griff had baked? It would have done the best bakeries proud.

As he set a big wedge of cake in front of me, I noticed that Snoopy and Dixie were watching through sliding glass doors that divided the area into kitchen and family room.

"They're spoiled," Griff said, nodding at the dogs. "If we let 'em in, they'll be in your lap."

"Are you still selling real estate?" I asked.

He shook his head and frowned. "Too many forms these days," he said. "It's no fun for an old man. Too complicated."

He had land in Nantahala that he was going to break up into lots, he said, but at 77, gardening and working in the greenhouse was all he cared to do.

"You all are so close to the mountains," I said. "Do you still notice them, or are you so used to them that you don't even see them?"

"No," he said, "all I've got to do is travel out of here and then I'm glad to be home. We went up north for a reunion, and my gosh the trucks and cars on the roads, the sirens, the noise, the traffic. . . . It was a treat to be back home. I'm spoiled. I love it . . . how sweet it is."

He clasped his hands and rested them on the table. "I'm a bigot," he said. "I like to live with my own kind."

Griff said that he and Ruth were Baptists. They didn't smoke or drink ("a waste of time," he said), and didn't have much use for TV. He liked classic movies and the History Channel; she watched the Atlanta Braves.

Griff said he "didn't watch a minute" of the reports on the 9/11 terrorist attacks. "I see that stuff on CNN and Headline News, and I don't believe a word of it," he said.

US foreign policy, he said, was "one-sided. I think we should mind our own business. All we seem to know is to bomb people. This is a good country—the best. I don't want to leave it, and you couldn't drag my wife out of it with a team of mules. But we're not the only good ones in the world."

Ruth took a pot of beans off the stove, drained it, and emptied it into a plastic freezer bag.

"We're having our annual early Thanksgiving in two weeks," Griff said, watching as Ruth sealed the bag. "We do it every year, third weekend in October. We invite the family while the weather's still nice and people can get outside. It's a large gathering. In November, it's too cold and the weather's not predictable."

During the winter, when the temperature can range from near zero to the 60s, they raise flowers in their greenhouse and sell them in the spring. "In March," Griff said, "there's usually a dry spell, and I like to plow my rye under then or it gets too tall."

"Do you have any other interests besides gardening?"

"I don't fish," he said, "and the one time I went hunting, I killed a deer and felt so badly about it that I didn't even bring it home. I gave it away."

If anything, it seemed like Griff and Ruth were a trifle lonely. Twice during my two-hour visit they invited me to come back for a weekend and stay with them. "We've got a lot of empty bedrooms," Ruth said. "We're rattling around in this place."

I thanked her and said I'd keep it in mind the next time I came back.

Other than wanting for visitors, Griff said they were about as happy as a couple could be.

"We've got an easy lifestyle," he said. "Easy. If I lived up north, I'd go nuts. People. Cars. People buying everything they eat from stores. . . . I couldn't live like that."

After finishing the cake, which was delicious, I thanked Griff and Ruth and told them I had to be on my way. They followed me out the door, and I assumed they were going to wave goodbye from the deck. But as I pulled away, I glanced back and they were deep in conversation, studying the garden below.

Chapter 22

Community

There had been one significant change in Andrews since my last visit, and it took place at the Bradley Inn. Jo and John Paul Jones had sold the place six months earlier to Greg Long, a hefty former fireman from Atlanta.

I met Long the next morning at Treats as he set a glutinous bowl of oatmeal in front of George Simmons.

"The coffee's free," he said, "but it's $26.50 for the ambience."

Once again, the bombing in Afghanistan was on everyone's mind. Freel and Caivano still could not accept that Ray Rowles disapproved of the raids. Rowles, a big, quiet retiree with silver hair and friendly eyes, was sitting at the far end of the table. Freel was to his left, Rev. Simmons to his right, and Caivano was next to Rev. Simmons.

"What're you gonna do, Ray?" Freel said, leaning forward and tapping Rowles on the shoulder. "Pat 'em on the back and thank 'em for bombin' our buildin's?"

"You know better than that," Rowles said. "I just don't think that the bombing's gonna solve anything."

"What would you do?" said Freel.

Rowles shook his head, perplexed. "I don't know."

To Freel and Caivano it was a clear-cut case of retaliation and vengeance. Anyone who attacked the United States had to be taught a lesson, an eye for an eye. But they liked and respected Rowles. It was evident in the way they deferred to him, and his position mystified them.

Rowles and Griff Griffing were two of the oldest men I'd met in Andrews, and both opposed the bombing. Neither was radical, and neither was eloquent. But their years offered what Thoreau called "the opportunity for wisdom," and in this case it wasn't popular. Whether it was vivid memories of Vietnam and the terrible cost there or something else wasn't clear, but Rowles wasn't budging.

There was a lot of rhetoric that morning, but the only noticeable shift came from Rev. Simmons. He said that although he had initially supported the bombing, he was rethinking his position.

It was a topic that was likely to arise again and again, like the sinking of Caivano's Jet Ski, and perhaps it never would be resolved. But that wasn't the point. Coffee at Treats was a ritual, and they would all be poorer without it. I think they understood that. Above all, it was heartening to see that friendships and fellowship transcended disagreements, or so it appeared.

When the others left, Greg Long sat down to explain how he had come to Andrews. It began at a car wash in an Atlanta suburb.

Long struck up a conversation with a stranger who happened to be John Paul Jones. Jones told Long that he and his wife had decided they wanted to move to Atlanta. Long said that he and his wife were disenchanted with life in Gwinnett County, at the time the fastest-growing county in the country.

Jones and Long exchanged phone numbers and went their separate ways. When Long got home that evening, he told his wife, Carol, about the conversation.

"I don't know if you believe in God or not," he said, pushing his glasses up on his nose, "but I do, and I believe there's no such thing as a coincidence. I believe I was meant to meet John Paul, just as I believe we're all here for a purpose."

The Longs decided to visit Andrews.

"It made no sense to leave the fire department," Long said. "I had three years left before retirement. We had a house with a pool, and I had said it was the last house we were ever gonna own. But here we are."

So the Longs and the Joneses swapped homes, communities, and lifestyles, and Long figured his family got the better of the deal.

"The thing that is really different, that nailed it down, is the people we met," he said. "The guys around this table. They are there any time we need them. It was like when I was growing up, people cared about you. They are interested in your life."

Not long after they settled in Andrews, Long bought a swing set for his three children. He commented the next morning at coffee that he'd hurt his back and couldn't put it up. It would have to wait until he recovered.

Caivano and Rowles showed up the next day and told him they were there to put up the swing set.

"I said, 'I can't do it today. My back still hurts,'" Long said. "They said, 'You'd just be in the way. Where do you want it?' They put that set up, and they wouldn't let me pay them or feed them or even give them something to drink. That's the kind of thing that happens here. People with other things to do do something for kids they don't even know that well. People do things for you without expecting anything in return."

Carol Long joined us at the table. She had just been to an exercise class with Rowles's wife, Jean.

"When we moved in, people came around and gave us hugs and brought us goodies," she said. "I told Greg I thought maybe we were going to die or something, because I've never been hugged so much in my life.

"The funny thing is, even though Greg was a fireman in Atlanta, for insurance reasons the kids weren't allowed to ride on a fire truck in parades. But two weeks after he joined the fire department here, the kids were on a fire truck."

The Long children, who were being homeschooled, were enjoying a life that might have been scripted by Booth Tarkington. They got to watch a circus tent being set up in a field on the other side of the four-lane. There was a birthday party at the library for Winnie the Pooh. The printer across the street let them watch him print.

Shop owner Beth Ann Elsberry had moved her shop to another town, but still lived in Andrews and became their unofficial grandmother. And one morning when he arrived for coffee, Caivano paused to applaud the kids for keeping their bicycles on the sidewalk.

Just the day before, I had walked past the small park next door to the inn and heard the Long children playing. The silvery sound of young voices at play was joyful and refreshing, an event full of promise right there on Main Street.

"Andrews is a great place," Long said. "I used to travel a lot, and the first time I came up here, I was thinking travel's nice, but it's not home. When we got to Andrews, there's that gazebo over in Hall Memorial Park, and my mom and dad were with us. I had the calmest feeling I've ever had: this was home. I'd never felt that before."

Chapter 23

Terrorists

George Simmons was outside the new activities building when I pulled up to St. Andrew Lutheran Church. Beard neatly trimmed, with hair carefully combed and wearing black clerical garb, he reminded me of Father Tim Kavanagh, an Episcopal priest in Jan Karon's novels about a mythical town in these same North Carolina mountains.

The long, low building had a fresh white façade and a broad, gabled roof. It contrasted vividly with the faded red-brick church next to it and just about everything else in the melancholy 800 block of Main Street.

Rev. Simmons led the way into the new building, which had a large multipurpose room in the center with smaller rooms to each side that included a kitchen, a conference room, and offices. But of all the new trappings, Rev. Simmons was especially proud of a long table in the conference room.

"I told the board we needed a table we could put all our papers on," he said, grinning. Then, as if to apologize for the extravagance, he added, "I decided to save a little money by not hiring a secretary."

We sat in easy chairs at a side table in the conference room, and I told him I was interested in his comment at coffee about rethinking the bombing in Afghanistan.

"How did you handle it with your congregation?" I asked.

"The Sunday after the attack, we sang 'My Country 'Tis of Thee,' and I talked about Dietrich Bonhoeffer," he said. Bonhoeffer, a Lutheran minister in Germany, was executed for his role in a plot to assassinate Adolf Hitler.

"Bonhoeffer thought Hitler was like a mad dog who had to be stopped," Rev. Simmons explained. "I saw this as a similar situation: we were facing acts we cannot understand. The government will pursue the terrorists, and their cause is just. War is horrible, but at times it is necessary. What else can you do?

"Then I read the presiding bishop's prayer, and we sang 'Mine Eyes Have Seen the Glory,' and we went on with our regular worship."

He spoke in calm, measured tones, as if aware that people and God were listening, and he wanted to be sure not to offend anyone. Still, he seemed uneasy.

"I didn't know what else to do," he said. "I even volunteered in case they needed a chaplain to serve with our servicemen and women."

"I've been to two gatherings of men at a church in Atlanta since the attacks," I said. "Each time I was surprised and impressed that only a few favored the bombing."

He pondered that for a few moments.

"You know, just yesterday an Air Force jet on a training run flew right over our house," he said. "That happens pretty often around here, but this one was so low and so loud that my wife thought it was going to crash into the house. It was one horrendous noise. Given what happened in New York, it was one scary experience."

He paused for a moment.

"I think we're pretty safe here," he said. "There are no crop dusters operating out of Andrews-Murphy Airport. But if terrorists had a plan to hijack a plane out of Atlanta, what happened in western Pennsylvania," where another plane hijacked by terrorists crashed, "could have happened in Andrews."

That Andrews could be the target of terrorists, or affected by terrorism, seemed pretty far-fetched, but only for a matter of hours. That afternoon, I picked up a copy of the Cherokee Sentinel & Business Report, a Cherokee County newspaper, and came across a fascinating article.

A businessman from Murphy named Don Whitener told the newspaper that just a few months before the 9/11 attacks, he saw two men at a small general-aviation airport in Copperhill, Tennessee. Copperhill is thirty-four miles from Andrews.

Whitener said the men arrived that day in a Cessna they had rented at an airport in an Atlanta suburb. He said they inquired about a number of nearby sites that included a chemical plant near Copperhill, the former Olympic kayaking venue on the Ocoee River in nearby Tennessee, and the Hiwassee Dam in Cherokee County, North Carolina.

They were told that the plant was virtually out of business, and its storage tanks were empty. They also learned that the Ocoee River was low much of the year and the kayaking venue was seldom used.

The dam, however, was very much in business. It impounds Hiwassee Lake and is used for flood control and to generate electricity. The lake is 22 miles long and in some places 200 feet deep. At 1,376 feet wide and 307 feet high, Hiwassee Dam is also the highest over-spill dam in the world. In addition, it is just nine miles from Murphy as the crow flies, and 20 miles from Andrews.

Whitener told the newspaper he was suspicious of the men but had nothing to go on other than the feeling that they were not trustworthy. When the 9/11 terrorists were identified, Whitener recognized two of them as the men he had seen at the Copperhill airport and contacted the FBI.

One of the men was Mohammed Atta, a 34-year-old Egyptian who coordinated the 9/11 attacks and piloted American Airlines Flight 11 into the north tower of the World Trade Center. Whitener said he believed the other man was Marwan Al-Shehhi, who flew United Airlines Flight 175 into the south tower of the World Trade Center.

Referring to Atta, Whitener told the Sentinel, "I'm 110 percent sure it was him. His eyes were two black holes."

Finally, no chapter on terrorists in the Smokies would be complete without mentioning that most elusive of woodland creatures, Eric Robert Rudolph.

As it turns out, just a few weeks before my return to Andrews in October 2001, a group of hikers in the Nantahala National Forest saw Rudolph not far from the Nantahala Outdoor Center.

I learned about the incident many years later from Emily Goins Smith. When I met Ms. Smith, she was the youth director at Northwest Presbyterian Church in Atlanta. In 2001, however, she was a counselor at Camp John Knox near Oak Ridge, Tennessee.

"I was a guide for a group of hikers that we brought down to the Nantahala Outdoor Center," she said. "I was 19 at the time and a student at Queens College in Charlotte. The other guide was Brie Payne. She was 22 and had just graduated from the University of North Carolina–Greensboro."

Emily and Brie had met at camp years before and become close friends. As counselors at Camp Knox, they often brought groups to the outdoor center and were familiar with the trails and campsites. On that particular trip, they had eight high school kids with them.

"We had rafted earlier in the day and were hiking up to a shelter to spend the night," Emily said. "We were on a trail that wasn't commonly used, and as we crested this ridge there's a guy halfway down the hill standing in the trail.

"As soon as he saw us, he locked eyes with us for a moment and then turned and went into the woods. The rhododendron along the trail was really thick, and the trail wasn't very wide, so a person could get into cover easily. Off to the right there was a kind of hollow formed by the ridge, and I could see that he'd made a shelter there."

She paused. "It put such a chill into me that it was unreal. I looked back at Brie and I could see she had the same feeling. We had to decide whether to go back or keep going. She kind of nodded, so I went ahead and we just booked it right through. But as soon as we got over the next ridge, we stopped and took a deep breath. We run into people all the time on the trails, but it's never like that. It was Rudolph. I've got chills right now thinking about it."

"Did you report seeing him?" I asked.

"We did when we got back to the center the next day, and they notified the police. They searched for him, but of course he was gone."

"What was he wearing?"

"Canvas pants and a green, long-sleeved shirt," she said. "And he was dirty. He looked like he'd been in the woods a long time."

She paused, picked up her phone, and called Brie Payne. She reminded Brie of that experience on the trail 20 years ago. Brie said, "It still gives me chills."

Visualizing that scene on the trail later, I wondered what it was about Rudolph that was so frightening. Obviously, he was capable of violence, but his targets had been abortion practitioners, lesbians, and in his cockeyed reasoning, socialists. Random hikers didn't fit his target profile, and by their very number a group of 10 hikers would seem to be safe.

On the other hand, Rudolph had been a hunted man for three years at that point. His diet must have been marginal and his accommodations spartan: no bed to sleep on, cave temperatures in the mid-50s, winter temperatures that could drop to zero, and in the warm months heat, humidity, insects, snakes, and assorted wildlife.

There were unconfirmed rumors that some local people helped Rudolph. While possible and even plausible given militants in the area, his appearance that day suggests that if he was getting help, it must have been brief and infrequent. Even for a misanthrope, it had to be a lonely, challenging existence.

I've spent a fair amount of time in nature and always found it soothing and restorative. But I always returned to the amenities of the everyday world. Deprive someone of civilization for three years, especially someone hiding in caves and hollows, probably armed and nursing a bad attitude, and you've got the makings of a feral human.

Running into someone like that would be a shock to the system. Eye contact doesn't seem like much, but it can be an immediate and powerful form of communication. No wonder Rudolph scared people.

Rudolph was eventually captured in 2003 while dumpster-diving behind a food store in Murphy. He pled guilty to multiple state and federal homicide charges and was sentenced to four consecutive life sentences in a federal maximum-security prison.

Chapter 24

Regular Guy

The last person I wanted to see on my farewell tour was Jim Dailey. I called him that afternoon, thinking he would probably refuse to see me. He had been front-page news in Andrews for nearly a year, and it was less than a month after his sentencing.

But he sounded pleased to hear from me and invited me to the house after dinner.

The air was still, and the early-evening sunlight slanting across the mountains lit up pockets of red, gold, and yellow, and threw long, dark shadows across hollows and valleys. I pulled off the road and stopped, hoping the image would burn itself into my memory, and wondered yet again if people in Andrews ever got tired of the mountains.

Dailey came out on the porch when I drove up. He wore jeans and a blue T-shirt, and his face was reddened by the sun. He looked younger and healthier than when I last saw him.

"Man, you look great!" I said.

"Thanks," he responded with a happy grin. "I've lost thirty pounds. C'mon in."

The first room inside the front door looked like it was meant to be a dining room as it opened into the kitchen. But the Daileys had turned it into a family room with a couple of couches, a recliner, a coffee table, and a brown and black rug.

In one corner was a freestanding gas fireplace, and against the front wall, between two windows, was a hutch with a TV tuned to a Major League Baseball playoff game.

"Are you still pouring concrete for Dick Strahan?" I asked.

He nodded. "It's a change of pace," he said. "It's good for me to get away from things. This whole thing has been hard on me and my family. The newspaper got on me pretty hard, and the way the case went, we couldn't plead guilty to some charges and not guilty to others. They charged us with things we didn't do, and we've got to pay money to the town. Some of the charges were items I planned to repay out of the overtime I had before I got fired."

He paused. "As the mayor, I was on call 24 hours a day," he said. "I'd get calls at three in the morning."

He picked up the remote and switched off the TV.

"It cost me $10,000 in attorney's fees," he said. "But it was worth it. Reid"—Reid Brown, his attorney—"did a good job, but I wish I could get my life back. It's been this way for over a year."

A condition of Dailey's probation was that for six months he had to be home by 6 p.m. and could not leave until 6 a.m. Every night, a probation officer drove over from Robbinsville, 30 minutes away, to make sure he was home.

"I told him he didn't have to worry about me," Dailey said. "I'm not going anywhere."

Dailey was also ordered to undergo periodic drug tests, a requirement that bordered on the absurd. His case had nothing to do with drugs, and as a devout Baptist, he didn't drink alcohol.

On the other hand, he had violated an oath and public trust and had admitted his guilt. Being drug-tested and confined to one's home overnight for six months beats the harsh reality of a jail cell.

The front door opened, and Dailey's wife came in. Sherry Dailey was a shy, petite, blue-eyed blonde several years younger than Dailey. During the trial she had testified that Dailey may have misused town money because she was pressuring him to finish their new home.

"I admire you for what you told the court during Jim's trial," I told her.

She blushed. "I wish I could have said more," she said, "but I got nervous and forgot what I wanted to say."

She glanced at Dailey. "We didn't get what we wanted," she said, "but I guess it turned out okay."

She looked at Dailey again. "I'm gonna get ready for church."

He nodded.

It was Wednesday evening, and the court-imposed curfew kept him from going to church on Wednesday and Sunday evenings, as was his custom. "That's the thing that hurts the most," he said. "Those people at church stood behind me. They helped me a lot."

Dailey's punishment also included 120 hours of community service, which he said he was fulfilling by working at the town landfill Thursdays, Fridays, and half a day on Saturdays.

"I could be working, building houses during that time," he began, then stopped and shrugged. Crime and punishment couldn't have been spelled out more clearly.

"I read what Dick Strahan said about you at the trial," I said. "That was pretty impressive."

Dailey bowed his head for a moment, then looked up. "Dick's a super-nice guy, the best I've ever worked for in my life," he said. "And you know what? I could go over to his house right now and go into his carport and take his car, and he would never ask me a question about it. I can't thank him enough for what he's done. I couldn't ever pay him back . . . and a lot of others in this town, too."

Dailey added that he thought certain members of the town council were "out to get me." He thought the whole affair could have been handled without bringing in the state Bureau of Investigation, sparing him and the town legal expenses.

"Bill and I tried to explain to the board, but they cut us off," he said. "It was politics. We didn't get a chance to tell our story. We made arrangements to pay everything back, but we didn't get a chance to do it.

"I about could write a book about the way the whole deal happened . . . seeing the good side and the bad of people," he said. "People you thought you could trust let you down. I learned that the hard way. My downfall was I was good to people."

Others could argue, as the district attorney had, that it was Dailey who let down people who trusted him by misusing town funds. But Dailey was not given to irony, so I asked what he meant.

"After I was fired," he said, "the council ordered the town employees not to talk to me. I thought that was uncalled for."

Dailey said he had done favors for some of the employees over the years and he couldn't imagine that they could turn their backs on him. It was ostracism, and in a town where conversation is the oxygen of everyday life, it was particularly humiliating.

But even before he'd lost his job, Dailey had been living a life that he could hardly call his own. It wasn't just the rumors and innuendo—some of which proved to be true. It was also the midnight calls and petty jealousies.

I'd had a glimpse of it during my first interview with Dailey when the scowling man with white hair and beard sat through the meeting without identifying himself or offering to leave. Whatever the cause, there was tension in the air. If friction was a regular occurrence in the mayor's office, Dailey had a right to feel beleaguered.

Reid Brown cast more light on the situation when he told the court that his client was an example of the Peter Principle—a good man who had risen beyond his capabilities and made mistakes.

But the healing that began in the courtroom with the show of support for Dailey continued afterward as well. Two weeks after the trial, Scott and Margaret Freel offered Dailey a job at Freel Builders Supply.

"I couldn't take it," Dailey said. "I felt I owed it to Dick Strahan to stay. But I know I can't go on pouring concrete, cleaning up construction sites, and doing odd jobs. I don't know what I'm going to do. I'll soon be 52, but right now I'm content. I'm more relaxed. I do my best to please the homeowner and Dick, and my day is complete. No meetings, no 2 a.m. phone calls, and when I lay down at night, God has given me peace. I don't have to worry."

He said he and Sherry had talked about selling their house and moving. "Not far away, because Andrews is home," he said. "But far enough where I can just be a regular guy."

Chapter 25

Home

In two days, I had connected with the people I wanted to see, checked to see how Andrews was doing at being Andrews, and it was nearly time to leave. But I had one more stop to make.

I drove out Pisgah Road to where it intersected with that gravel road, the place where I had stopped on that rainy evening more than a year earlier. I turned around on the gravel road, edged over to the left-hand side of the road and drifted to a stop, just as I had the first time.

I switched off the engine, lowered the windows, and composed myself, just as before. But not for long. A couple of cars drove past on Pisgah Road. Then a pickup pulling a trailer with roof joists rattled by, and not long after that a dump truck.

The weather wasn't encouraging either. It was cloudy and cold, which is hardly unexpected in the mountains in October. Wind rattled in the trees and swept brown and yellow leaves across the road.

I had been hoping for another transcendent experience, but all I could think about was an espresso. An espresso takes extra effort and an expensive machine too, and in those days you couldn't get an espresso in Andrews.

So I drove back down Pisgah Road into town, then out to the four-lane and traveled the fourteen miles to Murphy.

I found a coffee shop in Murphy's bustling downtown and sat at a table sipping the espresso and brooding. As far as I could tell, this would be my last visit to Andrews. I had enough material to write a story, so that wasn't what bothered me.

I kept wondering what would happen to Andrews. I felt a real affection for the place, and I wondered if maybe someday you'd be able to get an espresso there. Or if someone might build a casino or a fancy hotel or a Jack Nicklaus golf course so that travelers would come in off the four-lane because there was something they wanted to see or do right there in Andrews.

Then again maybe none of those things would happen. There were probably people who wouldn't mind that at all. People who didn't want the town overrun by strangers driving around with the windows up, talking on cell phones. People who didn't want traffic and lines at restaurants, or cookie-cutter housing developments popping up in empty fields.

Andrews wasn't perfect, and neither were the people who lived there. No doubt it could be stifling for nonconformists. There was no ethnic diversity to speak of, and it might never offer amenities that measured up to the natural surroundings.

So what was it about this out-of-the-way corner of the world that was so compelling? What was it that had such a hold on "a hick from Ohio" like Griff Griffing? Why would Freel share so much of his life with a stranger like me? Despite what he'd been through, why would even Jim Dailey say that if he moved, it wouldn't be far?

For that matter, why did the place have such a hold on me?

This was Appalachia. I had spent a lot of time there over the past 18 months. I had interviewed people I liked and was grateful to know. People had trusted me and shared enough of their lives that I had come to care about them and about this little town to which they were so devoted. They had treated me as if I were one of them.

"This is a small town, but it's more like family," Freel had said.

He was right, of course.

"You have to experience it," Jane Brown, the instructor at Western Carolina University, had told me. "It's a sense of place. It's got something to do with the mountains."

That was part of it: the experience, the feeling, the energy of the place. It was the changeless, inevitable presence of those comforting mountains that moved Greg Long, an Atlanta fireman, to say, "This is home."

It was Caivano shutting off his Jet Ski in the middle of a lake and listening to the wind, the splash of a fish, and that majestic, restorative silence. Federal agents were so charmed by Andrews that they cut firewood, cared for the elderly, visited the hospital, and gave their time and souvenirs to Cub Scouts.

Andrews was a place where respect and consideration prevailed, where morality, community, and good manners dominated. If it seemed nostalgic and slow, it was. If it seemed old-fashioned and dull, it could be that, too.

But the roots of many Americans are no more than a generation or two removed from places like Andrews. If American Heritage were to curate a town as a cultural theme park, Andrews would be a candidate.

And that's what touched me. It wasn't just about Andrews. It was about all those places where people live in community and every day demonstrate determination, kindness, generosity, and forgiveness.

Memories. Coffee with the regulars at Treats. The woman in the minivan who went out of her way to lead me to Griff's house. Visiting under the overhang at Freel Builders Supply on a rainy night. Bob McClure sitting in his garden like a sun-washed Buddha. The Long children playing in the park. A young bride crossing the street to a new life.

The clock on Caivano's wall, ticking.

Andrews may have suffered economically, but to those who managed to stay, it also offered the ultimate luxury—time. Time to stop and visit, time to go home for lunch, time to see the class play, time to wave at a passing motorist, time to admire the mountains. Time to reflect.

I finished the espresso, set the little cup on the table, and stared at it. Speaking of time, it was time to go back to Atlanta, to my cat, to my friends, to life in a city. It was what I did. It was who I was, and at the moment I wasn't looking forward to it.

I got up reluctantly and walked to the car. As I pulled out onto the four-lane, I couldn't resist a glance in the rearview mirror. I was headed for Atlanta, but it felt like I was leaving home.

Chapter 26

Welcome

When I returned to Atlanta, I wrote a long piece about my experiences in Andrews. It was too long for magazines, so I decided to give it a shot as a book. A very short book, admittedly, but a book nonetheless.

I sent the manuscript off to an agent suggesting that he find a publisher for it. The agent returned it without comment, which might be the worst kind of rejection. Left to my imagination and character defects—industrial-grade self-doubt, perfectionism, and waiting for the other shoe to drop—I could have come to the wrong conclusion and thrown it away.

I didn't. I knew I had something, I just didn't know what was missing. So I stuck the manuscript in an accordion file and forgot about it.

Over the next several years, I did all kinds of things for income, from freelancing for local newspapers (daily and weekly) and creating web content to conceptualizing a travel book and writing a résumé for a guy trying to get hired by Microsoft (he got the job). I even spent a month in a warehouse packaging Serengeti sunglasses for Overstock.com.

I contributed research to books about Martin Luther King Jr., Hurricane Katrina, and the Shepherd Center, a hospital specializing in spinal cord and other debilitating injuries, and that led to writing books. The first was a history of the Washington Tennis & Education Foundation in the nation's capital. The second was a nonfiction ebook about an eccentric golfer named Mike Austin. The first was a contract job and didn't pay much. The second was professionally edited but self-published, and paid even less.

Nothing I tried was as profitable or as comfortable as working for someone else, so I kept hoping that something else would show up and it did. The director of a media agency asked me if I'd ever done any acting.

If I'd been honest, I would have said, "Yeah, I've been faking it all my life."

I said no, of course. I was 59 years old, too late to be starting a new career. But this wasn't about finding the next Olivier. Advertisers were eager to reach baby boomers who were starting to show their age, and I looked like an aging baby boomer. My first agent (at one point I had three) took one look at my graying hair and said, "Don't do anything to your hair."

I did have to take acting lessons, but mostly I just had to show up. Over the next several years I appeared in more than forty commercials for companies like Bayer (Advil), Delta Air Lines, and Home Depot, and did one-off jobs for everything from a hospital in Memphis to a casino in Alabama and a resort in St. Thomas.

I appeared for a few seconds as a suit on a telecast of the People's Choice Awards. I was also the "featured extra" in a nonspeaking scene with Janet Jackson in the film Why Did I Get Married? The scene was cut, however, and my check for that 12-hour day, after taxes, was $66.78.

I was basically treading water financially, while major expenses (tires, a water heater, etc.) ate my savings. Eventually I was putting things on credit cards and doing the balance transfer tango.

But I wasn't the only one. A lot of people were out of work and hurting as the dot-com bubble deflated and was followed by the Great Recession. The term "financial security" was becoming a bad joke.

At one point, my situation was so precarious that I finally had to ask for help. That led to breakfast at a Waffle House with a guy I had befriended in a men's group at church. He gave me a check for $600 that was good immediately. I gave him a check for $600 that would be good in a few weeks.

He mentioned another men's group he belonged to and thought it might be helpful. I don't recall that he even mentioned its name at the time, but it turned out to be a 12-step program called Al-Anon. Al-Anon, which is not to be confused with Alcoholics Anonymous, is for the family and friends of alcoholics.

I didn't know any alcoholics and I wasn't sure I met the qualifications for the group. What kept me coming back was hearing a guy at that first meeting say, "I'm addicted to feeling shitty." I knew then I'd found my people. The implication was that, yes, he had issues and he was there to do something about them.

Within a few months I discovered that there was alcoholism on both sides of my family. I also found that the 12 steps were the best and most practical spiritual program I've ever encountered. I still feel that way.

But recovery takes time, and the pressure of declining income, the recession, and a persistent case of the blues led to another development that gave me hope—a visit with my physician.

Doctor: "Are you having any suicidal thoughts?"

Me: "I was, but they went away when I quit watching Atlanta Falcons games."

I got the laugh, but more important I also got a prescription for sertraline. The medication took the edge off my anxiety, but it didn't give me the lift that others talked about. Boosting the dosage helped, but then I couldn't sleep.

So I scraped along, always knowing I was a better person than I appeared to be, but unable to shake off the chains from the past. Fortunately, there were others who saw me in a better light.

"There's no way you should still be out there where you are, but you are," said my friend Robert. "God must have his hand on you."

In the spring of 2021, Amazon started something called Kindle Vella. The idea was that writers could post stories online an episode at a time and, if they chose, publish them later as books. The first few episodes would be free, but readers would have to pay to read the rest of the story.

The Andrews manuscript came to mind immediately. I could post a few chapters and see if there was any interest. If so, I'd post the rest of it. It might generate a little income and maybe even attract a publisher.

But reading over the manuscript, I realized why the agent sent it back. It wasn't complete. It was a collection of anecdotes looking for a story. One option would be to take a documentary approach. That is, do more research about Andrews, its history, and of course the people, and bring everything up to date.

That was not at all what I wanted to do, however, and fortunately I had already pointed myself in another direction. From the very first chapter about Andrews I had written in the first person. First-person reporting is not a rarity, but it's not something I had ever done. I did so in this case because virtually every anecdote in Andrews required my interaction with another person. It seemed like the most natural way to tell the story.

But the last chapter—"Home"—bothered me. Up to that point I'd been able to keep some distance from the narrative, but then I went deep by admitting my sadness about leaving Andrews. And the more I thought about the sadness, the more it baffled me. Why did Andrews feel like home? Why the sadness at leaving? And why did the sadness feel familiar? What was I missing?

I walked that puzzle around for days until I finally got the answer. When I was a child, we visited my grandparents' farm in Michigan. I loved the place. I played and climbed on everything, from the tractor and pickup to the chicken coop, the sloping roof of the barn, the cherry tree over the shed and a signaling platform down by the railroad tracks.

I rode on the tractor and in the back of the truck, and very briefly on the back of a horse. We went fishing. I rode with Grandfather when he took a truckload of cherries into town. I followed him around the barn when he did chores. When we left the farm after two weeks, I buried my face in the backseat so that no one could hear me cry. It was the only place I'd ever felt safe and free.

How curious, then, that the same feeling should arise in Andrews. Andrews wasn't my home any more than Scottville, Michigan, was. A trip to the dictionary gave me the answer: "home" isn't necessarily a building, town, or region. It can also be "a place where something flourishes."

I flourished on the farm, and five decades later I flourished in Appalachia, a region famous for its suspicion of strangers. I was treated with kindness and respect. People liked me and seemed to enjoy my company: coffee at Treats, lunches with Caivano and Freel, pie at Griff's place, Freel showing me his hideaway, kidding with Lawrence Hyde, Bob McClure's sense of wonder.

I banked a lot of memories in 18 months. The wonder is that it took 20 years to realize how much capital I'd built up. The things I had been searching for all my life—acceptance and understanding—were mine in Andrews without asking. And in response, without trying and without realizing it, I had showed up as much more like the person I always hoped I could be.

Danish theologian and philosopher Søren Kierkegaard wrote that while life must be lived moving forward, it is best understood looking backward. What was missing from the manuscript was me—my story. Twenty years later, I could see what I could not see when I was in Andrews— that "home" is not necessarily a place. It's also a feeling, a fullness, and an opening of the heart.

That freed my spirit, and over the next few months the chains I'd been dragging around for a lifetime broke away, one link at a time. It was nothing sudden, just steady, incremental improvement. To switch metaphors, it was like watching the sun rise, slowly and gently infusing me with a sense of joy and freedom.

Incidents that bothered me in the past no longer seemed so important. Thoughts that used to terrorize me diminished. I started showing up as an improved, more authentic version of myself.

I was more open and vulnerable. I admitted my mistakes. I made amends when I screwed up. I was less likely to criticize. I praised others. When I had an opinion or personal experience, I shared it without hesitation. That was new behavior that I seemed incapable of preventing, and sometimes it startled me. I'd get in my car afterward and think, "Did I just say that?"

I even took the ultimate male risk and told a lady friend that she'd hurt my feelings . . . and she didn't abandon me.

Going for a walk became a joy. I greeted men, women, children, and toddlers as family. I befriended cats and all kinds of dogs, from Goldendoodles to French Bulldogs, from a Great Dane named Harvey to West Highland Terriers named Alfie and Fezziwig (Dickens, anyone?) to a minivan-sized Newfoundland named Titan.

Invariably, I left those encounters feeling better than when they began.

I came across a definition of love one day from a Princeton Theological Seminary professor named James E. Loder: "Love is nonpossessive delight in the particularity of the other." The wording put a hitch in my stride, so I modified it to suit my own rhythm: "Love is the unconditional delight in the particularity of others."

Unconditional delight—love—is what I feel on those walks and in so many other venues, and it's an everyday miracle. The joy in connecting with others is remarkable. The generosity I feel toward others is, more than anything, an indication of how much I have changed.

I call those connections "turning on the lights" because it reminds me of getting out holiday decorations. You plug in a string of lights, replace the ones that don't work, and string them up. But you only leave them up for a week or two or a month, then put them away for another year.

For me, the lights may be metaphorical, but I don't turn them off and I don't put them away. We have connected. We are family. The lights stay on.

I always knew that love and kindness were inside me somewhere, but I couldn't let them out. I didn't know how, but I kept looking, kept trying new things, kept doing the footwork. I found that change at a personal level is possible, worth the effort and even magical, at times, but it takes perseverance.

The irony is that for so much of my life I was grasping and needy, looking for the secret, the answer, something that would bring me level with everyone else. Whatever it was, I knew that when I found it, I would keep the secret to myself and no one would ever know what a failure I used to be.

I was wrong. The goodness was always there waiting to be discovered, and what still amazes me is that when the heart opens, you can't keep it a secret. Nor do you want to, because the more you give away, the more you get. I don't want to go all holy roller here, but the lifelong search that led a pastor to call me a "wild card" finally led to acceptance that we are the children of a loving and generous creator. Appearances notwithstanding, we live in a friendly universe.

Epilogue

In the early 1970s, I was living in Louisville, Kentucky, and writing features for a weekly magazine published by The Louisville Times. I was in my late 20s, newly divorced and my ex had taken our daughters seven states away.

This was during the "sex, drugs, and rock'n'roll" era. Having married at 17 and become a father at 18, I had watched from the sidelines while everyone else was having all the fun and I was determined to catch up.

I lived in the Highlands, a leafy old section of town on the top floor of a three-story house. A few blocks away on Rosewood Avenue, there was a grand old building with six railroad-style apartments. The rooms were big, the ceilings high, and the detailing grand. It must at one time have been an impressive address for impressive people.

In my time, the grandeur was upstaged by countercultural levity. In four of those apartments, at any given time on any given day, you could be sure to find someone who was amenable to getting high.

On one such afternoon, eight men sat in a circle on the carpeted floor of a second-floor apartment. In the center stood a stocky Mexican man I'll call Pablo. At his feet was a duffel bag, and next to it a plastic bag of fragrant, resinous marijuana from Colombia.

Pablo was making a business call, and two things stand out about that afternoon.

First, Pablo had an air of violence about him. His was a high-risk occupation where being successful was not simply a matter of customer service. The penalties for selling marijuana were harsh. Getting it into the country from Mexico, Central America, and South America while evading border authorities, police, and hijackers was often high-adrenaline, action-figure work. The question wasn't whether there were firearms in Pablo's duffel, but how many.

The other thing was that I knew only four guys in that circle. Two were lawyers, one was a social worker, and one was Pablo's younger brother, whom I'll call Juan. Juan was a regular at Rosewood and Pablo's polar opposite—warm, mellow, and likable. I would have trusted Juan with my last dollar.

But the other four were strangers and my social filters—screening body language, attire, speech, and behavior—told me they were not the kind of people with whom I would ordinarily associate. Were it not for the aromatic buds at Pablo's feet, it was unlikely our paths would ever have crossed.

However, after a fat, deftly rolled sample made its way around the circle a few times, the group loosened up. Music was playing, conversation livened up, and restraints fell away. We found a way to be agreeable, communal, even convivial.

Credit the cannabis for breaking the ice, and at a certain point I had a surprising insight: whatever our differences, I had much more in common with the strangers than not. By sitting in a circle and sharing, we were perpetuating a custom as old as humanity itself. We were all members of the same tribe—the human tribe.

This is not a brief for smoking pot or drug use. I wasted a lot of time during those years, and all my issues were there waiting for me like a dog wagging its tail when I quit doing drugs.

But that tribal notion was profound and widespread in those days. It was a form of currency among young people, our own way of relating. It wasn't that our elders lacked empathy and generosity. It's just that their impulses were more studied and cautious. Their histories were fraught with challenges, their priorities elsewhere.

That tribal feeling is also what kept drawing me back to the Smokies, and shortly after my long-delayed awakening in the spring of 2021 I had an opportunity to experience it in yet another context.

On a chilly May evening, I was sitting by a fire pit in my brother Jeff's backyard in Connecticut. Also around the fire were his sons, Graham and Eric, and Graham's fiancée, Jamie, and a fourth person who has slipped through one of the gaps in my memory.

The occasion was heartbreaking. Earlier that day, we attended a funeral service for my nephew Jack, Graham's younger brother and Eric's fraternal twin. Jack died at age 27 from a rare and devastating genetic disorder called neurofibromatosis type 2.

Speaking at the service that morning, I commented that our far-flung family (five brothers, four sons, four daughters) had at one time or another lived in Spain, Hawaii, and Hong Kong and too many mainland US addresses to count. The inevitable consequence of such wandering was that I hadn't spent nearly as much time with Jack or anyone else in the family as I wished.

When the conversation around the fire drifted back to family, I found myself explaining my parents—the grandparents Graham, Eric and Jack never knew—and the family dynamic.

I told them about the alcoholism and the other things that generation had to deal with—World War II, the Korean War, the Cuban Missile Crisis, Vietnam, the recession of 1974, and possibly the most scarring event of all, the Depression.

"My experience is that they were not good communicators," I said. "They kept everything inside, but who could blame them? Who were they gonna complain to? Everybody in their generation went through the same things. Everybody was fearful or angry, or both."

I told them that after my father died at 59, my greatest regret was that he never told stories on himself. In particular I meant stories about screwing up, as he surely must have, and recovering from his mistakes, as he surely did. I told them I had spent most of my life trying to be as perfect as he pretended to be, and finally realized what a fraud perfectionism is. (Special thanks, by the way, to the wonderful Anne Lamott, who called perfectionism "a mean, frozen form of idealism.")

I told them that there is little to be gained from anger and blame, and the reasons good people give pain to others matter only to therapists and people who write books. Healing is about owning the past and moving on.

Sitting there in a circle, darkness surrounding us, faces orange in the fire's glow, I shared with them what my father could not share with me. I wanted them to have the opportunity to benefit from my mistakes, to be aware, to make good choices, to recover from their mistakes, to experience the joy of connecting and the freedom of vulnerability.

When I finished, Graham said quietly, "Thank you for sharing that with us."

I don't think I can explain how gratifying that experience was. I share it here because it answers the question: *"What do you do with the new you?"*

Self-realization is not a destination, it's a path to service.

The tribe—the human tribe—needs the wisdom and strength of its elders to shore up the hope and good intentions of younger generations. I stumbled onto that understanding that night by the fire, and it reminds me of the Pony Express, which carried the mail between Missouri and California in 1860 and 1861. Riders raced across the country on horseback carrying saddlebags filled with mail, stopping every 10 miles to change horses.

Decades of experience give elders the opportunity to be wonderful messengers, but we have to show up on "fresh horses." In particular, that means dropping the dismal "I'm getting old" mentality. No complaining, no grumpiness, no self-righteousness, and no "holier than thou."

There's a lot of ugliness in the world. It needs elders who are self-aware and have cleaned up their side of the street. It needs senior citizens sharing their wisdom the way elders of Indigenous tribes around the world did and, I hope, still do.

PAGE 191

"Getting old" is destructive and self-limiting. It is choosing to be a victim. Rather than retreating to gated communities, high-rise warehouses, and narrow self-interest, elders should share that beautiful and idealistic "peace and love" vibe to fortify the optimism, tolerance, and energy of the young.

Abundant research indicates that retirees without purpose die sooner than those whose senior years are filled with meaningful activity. I don't know that opening up and sharing with others will keep us young, but it might. There is no shortage of support for the power of the mind, from the biblical "As a man thinketh, so shall he be" to a line from Richard Bach's book Illusions: "Argue for your limitations, and they are yours."

When I was 62, a friend of mine who was six months younger than I commented, "We're getting old."

It pissed me off, and I had to think about it for several days before I got the answer. When I saw him again, I said, "We start aging as soon as we're born, but 'getting old' is a state of mind, and I refuse to go there."

Aging is ineluctable, a fact of life. Why not enjoy it? When I was in my 50s, I felt self-conscious about getting older and resisted giving my age. When I turned 60, I figured, Screw that, and took back the initiative. I told friends I wanted to have a party, and they obliged. We had another when I hit 70, and I've reached the point now where I hope people will ask how old I am.

So when a young guy obliged one afternoon at the YMCA, I told him I was 77. He was amazed, which of course I shamelessly encouraged. Then I added, "I can't wait to see what I'm like when I grow up."

He laughed, which is exactly what I wanted him to do, but I wasn't kidding.

CPSIA information can be obtained
at www.ICGtesting.com
Printed in the USA
JSHW060943150523
41722JS00006B/253